Asian Monsters

28 Terrifying Serial Killers
from Asian and the Far East

Robert Keller

**Please Leave Your Review of This Book At
http://bit.ly/kellerbooks**

ISBN-13: 978-1544000343

ISBN-10: 1544000340

Table of Contents

Tsutomu Miyazaki

On the afternoon of August 22, 1988, four-year-old Mari Konno left her home in Saitama, Japan, to play at a friend's house. When she had not yet returned by 6:30, her father went looking for her. Failing to locate his daughter, the panic-stricken man called the police to report her missing. A massive search was launched but to no avail. The child in fact lay dead in a forest 30 miles away, the first victim of Tsutomu Miyazaki, one of the most depraved serial killers in Japanese history.

Tsutomu Miyazaki was born in Itsukaichi, Tokyo, on August 21, 1962. He was a premature baby, entering the world at just over four pounds. He also had a birth defect. His hand joints were fused together, making it impossible for him to bend his wrists upwards.

Miyazaki grew to be a lonely child, shunned by his peers, mostly ignored by his parents and abhorred by his two younger sisters. Despite this he did well at school, at least at first. By the time he reached high school he'd lost interest in his studies and had retreated into a fantasy world, fueled by Manga comic books. He eventually graduated from Meidai Nakano High School, but the obviously intelligent boy finished only 40th in a class of 56.

After school Miyazaki attended junior college, graduating in 1983 with a qualification that enabled him to work as a photo technician. He found employment at a printing plant owned by a friend of his father.

Miyazaki was still living at home, but the only family member with whom he shared a close relationship was his grandfather Shokichi. The lack of familial interaction drove him to other pursuits. He was still obsessed with Manga and Anime, but now he also began collecting violent videos and pornographic magazines. By 1984 he'd given up on adult porn and had fixated entirely on child pornography.

The trigger that set Miyazaki on his murderous path occurred in May 1988 with the death of his only friend in the world, his grandfather. Psychologists who later examined Miyazaki believe that this marked the breaking of his final bond with society. He turned ever inward, to his comics and videos and pornography. Soon he would turn to murder.

The first child to fall victim to Miyazaki was Mari Konno. The little girl's disappearance caused massive public distress in Saitama, an area unused to violent crime. Police cars with loudspeakers patrolled the streets warning parents not to allow their children out of their sight. Meanwhile the police spent nearly 3,000 man-days interviewing people who lived near Mari's home. They distributed 50,000 missing person posters and brought in tracking dogs in the hope of picking up a scent. Nothing.

A couple of people did report seeing Mari in the company of an adult man and the descriptions they gave, about 5-foot-six with a pudgy face and wavy hair, were accurate, but the information led nowhere. When the police received a genuine clue – a postcard sent to Mari's mother with the cryptic message "There are devils about" – they dismissed it as a hoax.

Six weeks after Mari Konno's disappearance, Miyazaki was driving through Hanno, Saitama Prefecture when he spotted 7-year-old Masami Yoshizawa walking along a road. He coaxed her into his car, drove to the hills near Komine Pass and strangled her. Then he stripped the child and sexually abused her corpse, leaving the body just 100 yards from where Mari Konno's decomposing body lay.

Masami was reported missing later that night and search parties quickly fanned out across the area. The following day thousands of posters were distributed, again to no avail. Masami's home was only eight miles from Mari's, leading the police to suspect that the two disappearances might be connected. But with no bodies and no clues, they were treating it as a missing person's case. It would not be the last.

On December 12, 1988, four-year-old Erika Namba was returning from a friend's house in Kawagoe when Miyazaki coaxed her into his Nissan sedan. He drove her to a park in Naguri where he instructed her to undress in the back seat. He then started photographing the child but after a car drove past, he panicked and strangled her.

Miyazaki wrapped the body in a sheet, put it in the trunk of his car and drove off. A few miles down the road the Nissan's front wheel slipped into a gutter. Miyazaki was stuck and terrified of being caught with the child's corpse in his trunk. Panicked, he carried the body into the woods and hid it.

When he returned there were two men standing beside his car. Between the three of them they managed to maneuver the vehicle back onto the road, whereupon Miyazaki slid in behind the wheel and raced off, without so much as a word of thanks to his benefactors.

The following day a forestry worker found Erika's body in the woods. The police had no doubt as to what they were dealing with now. A serial killer was stalking the children of Saitama.

As the news of Erika Namba's murder broke, the two men who had helped Miyazaki with his car came forward. But they incorrectly identified the vehicle as a Toyota Corolla, thus depriving the police of their most valuable lead to date.

So far Tsutomu Miyazaki had murdered three little girls, inflicting untold grief on their loved ones. As if that weren't enough, he began stalking the victims' families, calling them at all hours then saying nothing on the other end of the line. When the distraught parents stopped picking up the phone, Miyazaki would allow it to continue ringing for upward of 20 minutes. Eventually he tired of taunting the grieving families by telephone and resorted to more sickening measures.

A week after Erika Namba's murder, her father received a postcard with a message formed from cutout magazine letters: "Erika. Cold. Cough. Throat. Rest. Death." Then on February 6, 1989, Mari Konno's father returned from work to find a box on his doorstep. It contained

ashes, dirt, charred bone fragments and ten infant teeth. It also
contained photographs of Mari's shorts, underwear and sandals. There
was a note in the box. It read: "Mari. Bones. Cremated. Investigate.
Prove." The bones and teeth would later be identified as coming from
Mari Konno. Her case was now officially a homicide.

The box containing Mari's remains at last provided police with a
couple of substantive clues. The camera that had taken the photos was
identified as a Mamiya 6x7, a type used almost exclusively by printers.
In addition, the box was found to be of the type used to ship camera
lenses and the typeface on the postcard was determined to have come
from a phototypesetter. And yet amazingly, the police failed to take
action on these leads, when an investigation into local printing shop
employees might have snared their man.

And Miyazaki wasn't done yet with his sick game of taunting the
Konno family. They returned from Mari's funeral to find a letter
labeled "Confession." This sickening missive turned out to be a
detailed description of the changes Miyazaki had observed in Mari's
corpse.

"Before I knew it," he wrote, "the child's corpse had gone rigid. I
wanted to cross her hands over her breast but they wouldn't budge.
Pretty soon, the body gets red spots all over it. Big red spots, like the
Hinomaru flag. Or like you'd covered her whole body with red hanko
seals. After a while, the body is covered with stretch marks. It was so
rigid before, but now it feels like it's full of water. And it smells. How
it smells. Like nothing you've ever smelled in this whole wide world."
The Konnos handed the note over to the police. It got them no closer
to catching the killer.

On June 1, 1989, Miyazaki was driving near the Akishima Elementary
School when he spotted two small girls playing. He stopped and
started talking to them, eventually convincing one of the girls to take
off her panties. He was photographing the child when neighbors
spotted him and chased him off.

This close call did nothing to discourage Miyazaki. Five days later he
claimed his fourth victim.

On June 6 Miyazaki found five-year-old Ayako Nomoto playing alone
in a park in Ariake. He talked the child into posing for photographs for
him, then lured her to his car. His plan was probably to drive her to his
preferred killing ground but after the girl made a comment about his
misshapen hands, he struck out in a rage and strangled her. He then
drove home with the body in his trunk, stopping on the way to hire a
video camera.

Over the next three days, Miyazaki photographed and videoed the
child's corpse in a number of explicit poses. Then after the smell of
putrefaction became too much to bear, he hacked the body apart,
hiding the torso in a public toilet and the head, arms and legs in the
woods. He also kept some of the flesh, roasted it in his back yard and
ate it.

Five days later Ayako Nomoto's torso was discovered in the toilet. But
even now the police had no clue as to the man they were hunting. It
would take a private citizen to eventually bring Miyazaki to justice.

On Sunday, July 23, 1989, Miyazaki spotted two sisters playing in a
public park in Hachioji. He pulled over and cajoled the younger of the

girls to walk with him to a nearby river, instructing the older girl to stay behind. She immediately ran home to fetch her father who returned to find Miyazaki taking photographs of his naked daughter. The man attacked Miyazaki but he managed to break free and flee. The man then called the police and they apprehended Miyazaki as he tried to return to his car.

Originally charged with "forcing a minor to commit indecent acts," Miyazaki broke down 17 days later and confessed to the murders of Mari Konno, Masami Yoshizawa, Erika Namba and Ayako Nomoto.

Tsutomu Miyazaki was subjected to a barrage of psychological tests and finally declared responsible for his actions and fit to stand trial. On April 14, 1997, he was found guilty of murder and sentenced to death. He was executed by hanging on June 17, 2008.

Duan Guocheng

The Red Dress Killer

At around midnight on a sultry Thursday evening in 2001, 41-year-old Wang Guiyu was walking to her home in Wuhan, an industrial city in the east-central province of Hubei, China. Wang knew the neighborhood well so she cut through a series of back roads and darkened alleys. Still, she trod carefully. These streets were far from safe at night. Just recently there'd been rumors of a number of knife attacks on women. She was glad to eventually see the steel security gate of the middle-class apartment block where she lived.

Wang hurried across the street and then stopped to enter her access code. In the next moment she heard faint footfalls. Tensing at the sound, she started to turn. It was then that something heavy collided with the back of her head. Wang stumbled forward screaming, trying desperately to pull herself through the gate. She didn't make it. Gaining a handhold on her arm, her assailant spun her around and plunged a knife repeatedly into her chest, delivering seven brutal blows. Then as lights began to come on in the apartment building he fled, leaving the woman bleeding to death on the sidewalk.

Wang Guiyu was one of six women who fell to a vicious serial killer in the city of Wuhan during a frenzied three months in the summer of 2001. The night after her murder the killer struck again, dragging down a 20-year-old migrant worker and hacking her to death.

And yet it might all so easily have been avoided. In fact, the police in Yueyang just 80 miles away, knew exactly who was committing the murders and had passed this information on to their Wuhan colleagues. The Wuhan police had simply not paid attention.

Earlier that year in February 2001, six police officers had arrived at a cramped three-bedroom apartment in Yueyang. They were looking for Duan Guocheng, a 29-year-old security guard who lived there with his parents. Duan wasn't home so they sat down to wait, ignoring Hu Yunxiang's pleas to tell them what her son had done wrong.

The officers waited all night until Duan eventually appeared in the early morning hours. Spotting the policemen he fled and although the officers gave chase he managed to evade them. The officers then returned to the apartment and revealed to Duan's parents why they were there. Their son was wanted on nine counts of murder.

The police were convinced that Duan had fled the city. Immediately they transmitted bulletins to neighboring regions providing details of their suspect, along with a photo and a list of aliases that he might be using. They didn't hold out much hope though. Chinese police departments were notoriously insular. In all likelihood their bulletin would be ignored.

The Yueyang police were right about Duan leaving the city. But he hadn't gone far, just 80 miles down the road to Wuhan, a jurisdiction full to overflowing with migrant workers, the perfect hunting ground for a serial killer. He'd only been in the city a couple of months when he picked up the threads of his murderous campaign.

Just after midnight on May 7, 2001, a young woman was stabbed to death while on her way home from work. The following day another woman died and over the next month six more were attacked, four of them succumbing to their injuries. One of those fatalities was Wang Guiyu.

With the body count climbing, the Wuhan police scrambled furiously to catch the killer. A task force of over one thousand officers was put together; detectives leaned hard on their contacts; undercover female cops walked the streets hoping to lure the killer into the open. None of it helped. The Red Dress Killer (so named because he appeared to target women dressed in clothes of that color) continued to claim victims at will. It was as though the police were hunting a phantom.

Part of the problem was the lack of public awareness of the crimes. An informed public would have been alert to the killer and might have passed on valuable information to the police. But newspapers in China generally report on crimes only after the perpetrator has been caught so the dailies carried no stories about the murders, leaving the populace blissfully unaware of the savage creature in their midst.

On August 10, three months after the killings began, the Wuhan police finally decided to contact their colleagues in neighboring cities. From Yueyang they learned about Duan Guocheng, whose details had been sent to them back in February before the murders had even started.

According to the original bulletin, Duan often used the alias Hu
Cheng. Following that lead the police traced him in just three days.

To the embarrassment of the Wuhan police department, Guocheng was
found staying at a guesthouse called the Aerospace Institute Inn just a
few blocks from Wuhan's main police station. A unit was dispatched
to the hotel and after a brief struggle, took the killer into custody.

Duan Guocheng was charged with murder and went on trial in
December 2001. In February 2002 he was found guilty and sentenced
to death. Details of his execution are not recorded but Chinese justice
moves swiftly. He is likely to have been put to death soon after.

Mohan Kumar

From India comes the chilling tale of Mohan Kumar, a primary school teacher turned Bluebeard serial killer. This astonishing case first came to the attention of the Indian authorities in 2009 with the disappearance of a young woman named Anitha from the village of Bantwal Taluk.

The Indian police deal with countless missing persons reports every year and when the victims are poor and without influence or connections, these cases seldom receive the attention they deserve. In this instance however, the girl's parents were so sure that she'd met with foul play that they approached a local Hindu organization for help. The organization's elders then put pressure on the police to take action. Their inquiries would uncover an incredible web of deceit that had claimed the lives of at least 20 young women between 2005 and 2009.

The Bantwal police began their investigation in the obvious place. They subpoenaed Anitha's cell phone records and started working through the list. Still convinced that the girl had run off with a lover, they were astonished to find that one of the numbers Anitha had called belonged to a girl who'd recently been found dead in a toilet at a Mysore bus station. When Anitha's parents failed to recognize the girl's name and insisted that Anitha hadn't known her, the police had the first inkling that they might be onto something bigger than a mere missing person's case.

Obtaining the dead girl's cell phone records, they compared them to Anitha's and picked up one common number. It belonged to a 46-year-old former schoolteacher named Mohan Kumar.

Kumar was pulled in for questioning, with the police certain that he'd provide a rational explanation for his name being on the phone records of the two dead women. Instead he launched into an incredible tale of murder, lust and betrayal.

Kumar said that he'd started killing after he lost his teaching job in 2003. Desperate for money and unable to find employment, he'd hit on the idea of robbing and killing young women. His method was simplicity itself. He targeted only victims from lowly socio-economic backgrounds, whose disappearances or deaths were unlikely to cause a stir. He also focused on women in their late twenties or early thirties who he believed would be desperate to find a husband.

Once the smooth talking Kumar spotted a likely target he'd approach her in a public place, usually with the well-worn pickup line: "Do I know you? I'm sure I've seen you somewhere before."

He'd then strike up a conversation with the woman, presenting himself as an eligible bachelor even though he already had two wives and was divorced from a third. If the woman appeared susceptible to his charms, he'd ask if he could see her again. At the second meeting he'd declare his love and broach the subject of marriage. All but a few of the women blushingly accepted his proposal. Like any predator, Kumar had a talent for sniffing out the naive and incautious.

In India the bride's family is required to pay a dowry consisting of cash, jewelry and household goods. But the gallant Mohan declared that he was prepared to forfeit such worldly possessions in the name of love. He asked only that his lady-love elope with him immediately and that they marry in secret. A few of the women baulked at this suggestion but most were easily duped.

With the elopement now agreed upon, Kumar would arrange for his fiancée to meet him the next day at a temple in a neighboring town. He'd tell her to wear her best jewelry for the ceremony and also to bring along any cash and savings books that she might have. The women invariably complied, some even borrowed additional items of jewelry from friends and neighbors.

The sham ceremony would be performed by some unsuspecting priest. Afterwards Kumar would whisk his new bride away to a lodge or hotel where they'd spend the night and consummate their union. Little did the unfortunate woman know that the honeymoon was also her last night on earth.

The following morning Kumar would claim that he had some business to attend to and would ask the woman to walk with him to a nearby bus station. Before leaving he'd instruct her to remove all her jewelry and valuables and give them to him for safekeeping. On reaching the bus station he'd hand the woman a powder, insisting that she take it. It was a contraceptive he'd say, which she needed to take because they'd had unprotected sex the night before.

Trustingly the woman would retire to the public bathroom to swallow the powder, not knowing that it was cyanide. Within minutes she'd be dead and Kumar would ride out on the next bus, carrying her cash and jewelry with him.

Kumar had killed women by this method at the Mysore, Madikeri, Bangalore and Hassan bus stands as well as at the Kollur temple. And yet despite the remarkable similarities between the deaths, the police had failed to investigate. The prevailing belief was that the young women had taken their own lives over the breakup of a relationship. Who knows how many more would have fallen victim to the lethal Bluebeard if Anitha's parents had not pressured the Bantwal police into taking action.

Justice however was slow in coming. Mohan Kumar's much delayed trial eventually came before a judge in December 2013. Found guilty on three counts of murder he was sentenced to death. He currently awaits execution.

Hiroshi Maeue

The Suicide Website Murderer

The idea of a suicide website might seem bizarre to most westerners but in Japan, a nation with the highest per-capita suicide rate in the industrialized world, such sites proliferate. The concept is simple. Individuals intent on ending their lives post messages looking for others to support and comfort them through the process. Once contact is established they'll exchange e-mails, eventually agreeing on a time and place to meet. Two or more people then end their lives together, usually by asphyxiation. The method recommended on most of these sites is to light an antique charcoal burner within the confines of a closed motor vehicle.

In 2005 a killer began stalking the website boards. Hiroshi Maeue was 27 years old, a native of Sakai, Osaka Prefecture, with a strange affliction. He could not achieve sexual arousal unless he was strangling someone.

This obsession had already gotten him into trouble. In 1995 he'd been expelled from the Kanazawa Institute of Technology after he'd throttled a male friend into unconsciousness. In 2001 he'd been arrested for strangling two women. Neither of the victims had died but Maeue had been convicted of criminal assault and sent to prison for a year. Released in April 2002 he was soon in trouble again, this time for strangling a high school student. The boy recovered. Maeue was sent back to prison for two years.

No one knows when, or why Hiroshi Maeue struck on the idea of trolling suicide websites for potential victims. Perhaps in his warped thinking, he was doing no wrong since these people wanted to die anyway. Whatever the case, by 2005 he was a regular on the various chat sites. It was on one of these pages that he first encountered 25-year-old Michiko Nagamoto in February 2005.

Maeue quickly struck up a discourse with the young woman, exchanging twenty e-mails with her before he suggested that they meet. By then he had managed to convince her that he too had decided to take his own life. Perhaps recognizing a kindred spirit in Maeue, Nagamoto agreed to the meeting.

Michiko Nagamoto disappeared on February 19, 2005, sparking a massive police search which ultimately came up empty. Maeue would later confess that he lured the woman into a rented car on the pretense of ending their lives together. Once inside he turned on her, grabbed her by the throat and strangled her to death, achieving an orgasm as Michiko breathed her last. Later he drove to Kawachinagano, a mountainous area in the Osaka Prefecture, and buried her on the banks of a river.

Over the next four months Maeue managed to lure two more victims from the website. In May he strangled to death a 14-year-old Kobe schoolboy. In June he killed a male college student aged 21.

But unfortunately for Maeue his online activities had left a trail. Detectives looking into the disappearance of Michiko Nagamoto picked up the series of e-mails that had passed between the two and pulled Maeue in for questioning on August 5, 2005.

Once in custody, it did not take much to coax a confession out of Maeue. He seemed almost eager to share details of the three deaths he'd caused. The sight of another person "suffering in agony" thrilled him he said. He became sexually excited witnessing their death throes. And if the police had any reason to doubt his confession, he willingly led them into the mountains of Kawachinagano and pointed out the shallow graves of his victims.

Hiroshi Maeue went on trial at the Osaka District Court in March 2007. Found guilty on three counts of murder, he was sentenced to death by hanging. He subsequently instructed his lawyers not to appeal the sentence, saying that he deserved to die for what he had done.

He was hanged at the Osaka prison on July 28, 2009.

Saeed Hanaei

The Spider Killer

To most westerners Iran is a closed shop, a country run according to
the strict tenets of Islam, where crime and immorality are unheard of.
It might surprise you to learn therefore, that Iran has a serious problem
with drugs and prostitution, the former in the shape of opium pouring
over the border from neighboring Afghanistan, the latter in desperate
drug addicted women prepared to do anything to pay for their next fix.

In 2000, one man decided to do something about the problem.

Saeed Hanaei was a 39-year-old construction worker living in a
working-class neighborhood in Masad, one of Iran's holiest cities. By
all accounts he was an unremarkable man, married with three children.
He had served in the 1980-1988 Iran-Iraq War.

Then in 2000 an incident occurred that transformed Hanaei from a
loving father and husband to a brutal killer. While walking home from
the market, his wife was mistaken for a prostitute and propositioned by
a taxi driver. When Hanaei heard about the incident he flew into a rage
and swore vengeance.

At first he began harassing the men who cruised for streetwalkers in
his neighborhood. But that only got him beaten up so he turned his
attention to the women themselves. Now though, his revenge went
way beyond harassment.

Over the next year 19 women were found dead on the streets of
Masad. Each was a known prostitute. Most were drug users. Each had
been strangled with her own headscarf and wrapped in her chador, the
flowing black garment that covers a woman from head to toe.

As the body count mounted word began to spread about the so-called
"Spider Killer," sparking furious debate across the country. In more
conservative circles the murderer was hailed as a folk hero, someone
who had taken it upon himself to clean the streets of immoral women.

Iranians of a more progressive bent though, voiced fears that an
extremist religious group might be behind the slayings and accused the
police of laxity in pursuing the killer.

Whether that was true or not, the mounting death toll could not be
ignored and the police were forced into action. They began by
removing over 500 prostitutes from the streets as a 'safety measure.'
Then they launched a major operation to catch the killer. Saeed Hanaei

was arrested after an intended victim escaped and reported him to the police.

In custody, Hanaei had no problem in admitting to the murders. In fact he appeared proud of what he'd done and seemed to relish the adoration directed at him from various extremist groups.

"They were as worthless as cockroaches to me," he boasted. "Toward the end, I could not sleep at night if I had not killed one of them that day. It was as though I had become addicted to killing them."

According to Hanaei, he would go cruising for prostitutes whenever his wife and three children were away. He'd bring the women back to his home where he would strangle them and then dump their bodies on the streets or in open sewers. With some of his later victims, he'd even waited around for the body to be discovered and then helped the police load the corpse into the ambulance.

Had that been the full extent of Hanaei's confession, had he convinced the trial judges that his motivation had been based on religious conviction, he might well have received a lenient sentence. But he foolishly admitted to having sex with the victims before killing them and that admission lost him a lot of support. It surprised no one when he was found guilty of murder and sentenced to hang.

Saeed Hanaei was put to death at Masad Prison on April 16, 2002. Reportedly, he went to the gallows kicking and screaming. He had believed right until the end that his powerful supporters would get his conviction overturned.

Robert Keller

Javed Iqbal

In early December 1999, a letter arrived at the Daily Jang newspaper in Lahore, Pakistan. "I have sexually assaulted 100 children before killing them," it read. "All the details of the murders are contained in a diary that has been left at my home. This is my confessional statement."

A near-identical letter had arrived at Lahore's main police station earlier that same day but the authorities had paid scant attention to it (later reports would suggest that the inspector involved crumpled it up and threw it in the wastebasket). It was only once the police heard that the newspaper had sent reporters to the address that they responded. Within minutes, units were racing through the crowded streets of Lahore with sirens wailing.

By the time the cops burst into the small apartment the reporters were already there, standing gape-mouthed and ashen-faced among the carnage. There was blood on the walls, bloody handprints on the doorjamb. On the floor lay a length of chain, also encrusted with blood. Five large plastic bags were stacked against a wall, full to overflowing with children's shoes (85 pairs by a later count). More bags contained over a hundred children's clothing items. Then there were the photographs, piles of them, each documenting a victim in the moment before death, some of the boys as young as nine.

Each of these displays had been carefully arranged, a neatly stenciled sign tacked to the wall explaining its significance, as though the killer had turned his home into a macabre museum.

But the worst was yet to come. In the corner of the room stood a vat of acid, in which partially dissolved human remains bobbed near the surface. "The bodies in the house have deliberately not been disposed of so that the authorities will find them," read the placard above this exhibit.

As the police began reading the journals left behind by the killer, the sheer magnitude of the crimes came to light. He was claiming to have murdered 100 young boys aged between nine and fifteen years old. What is more, he'd carried out his killing spree in just five months.

Now the hunt was on to find the killer. He'd identified himself in his letters as Javed Iqbal.

Javed Iqbal was born in Lahore, Pakistan in 1956, the pampered child of a wealthy merchant. From his teenage years he began surrounding himself with a small army of young boys, luring them with his ready supply of cash and his 200cc motorcycle. He also wrote hundreds of letters to adolescent pen pals, later striking up friendships with those he deemed "attractive."

In 1980 Iqbal was arrested for sodomizing a teenager, although the charges were later dropped. Thereafter his family began pressuring him to marry; perhaps believing that matrimony would curb his inner demons. Iqbal did eventually get married in 1983 but the union lasted only two months.

Over the next decade Iqbal started a number of businesses, all of them aimed at attracting adolescent boys. First there was a video games store, then a tropical fish emporium and then a gymnasium. He even opened a school although it closed soon after, as parents were aware of Iqbal's reputation and refused to send their sons there.

Any financial loss that Iqbal incurred due to the closing of his school was recouped when his father died in 1993 and he inherited a hefty share of the 3.5 million rupee estate. He splurged on a large house and several cars. He also opened another video games store, this one larger than any he'd owned before.

In September 1998 Iqbal was attacked by two of his former victims and severely beaten. He was rushed to Lahore General Hospital where he remained in a coma for 22 days. Upon his eventual discharge he laid a complaint of robbery, claiming that the boys had stolen 8,000 rupees from him. However the police dismissed his complaint. To add insult to injury, they charged Iqbal with sodomizing the two youths.

Worse was to come for Javed Iqbal. The cost of his medical treatment was expensive and as none of his family was prepared to help him pay for it, he was forced to sell his house, cars and businesses. In the midst of all this his mother died, which Iqbal claimed was due to the stress surrounding his hospitalization and subsequent arrest.

Bitter and angry, reduced within months from a wealthy man to a pauper, Iqbal swore vengeance. He would kill 100 young boys he decided, revenge for the death of his mother and the perceived injustices dealt to him by society.

Working with four young accomplices – Sajid Ahmad, 17, Mamad Nadeem, 15, Mamad Sabir, 13, and another youth known only as Billa – Iqbal began luring young victims from Lahore's Minar-e-Pakistan Square in May 1999.

Convincing them to come back to his apartment was easy. The streets of Lahore, like those of all Pakistani cities, literally teem with unwanted and abandoned children. These urchins earn their meager living by begging, stealing, selling trinkets or offering massages. Most are starving and desperate to earn a few rupees to feed themselves or their families.

Once inside his home, Iqbal would drug them, sodomize them and strangle them with a length of chain. He and his accomplices would then cut up the bodies and dissolve them in a vat of acid before dumping the residue in a local river. One hundred boys met their fate this way and the authorities were not even aware that they were missing.

Now though the case was causing a huge uproar, with the public directing most of its anger at the corrupt and incompetent Lahore police department. Spurred into action, the cops launched the biggest manhunt in Pakistani history.

Iqbal had stated in his letter that he intended committing suicide by tying himself to a rock and throwing himself into the Ravi River. But the police dragged the waters without finding a body.

Meanwhile Iqbal's four young accomplices had been picked up in Sohawa after they tried to cash an 18,000-rupee travelers' check. Subjected to brutal police interrogation during which one of them, Billa, died, they failed to give up Iqbal's whereabouts. It appeared they genuinely didn't know where he was.

In the meantime Iqbal remained at large and might well have done so indefinitely had he not decided to give himself up. On December 30, 1999, with police across the country hunting him, he walked into the offices of the Daily Jang and calmly surrendered.

Iqbal and his three surviving accomplices were tried for murder in early 2000. During a grueling trial which included testimony from 102 witnesses, Iqbal changed his story. He now claimed that he had killed no one, that the entire thing had been an elaborate hoax aimed at drawing attention to the plight of street children.

The court wasn't buying it. On March 16, 2000, Judge Allah Bakhsh Ranja handed down a sentence of death, ordering that Iqbal be strangled with the same chain he'd used to kill his victims. His body was then to be cut into 100 pieces and dissolved in acid.

The older of Iqbal's accomplices also received a death sentence, while the two younger boys were sentenced to life in prison.

The barbaric sentence sparked outrage from human rights organizations around the world and even conservative religious groups within Pakistan condemned it. The sentence however, would never be carried out.

On October 8, 2001, officials at the Kot Lakhpat Prison announced that Iqbal and his accomplice Sajid had been found dead in their adjacent cells. The official version was that they had hanged themselves with bed sheets, although an autopsy would later reveal that they'd been severely beaten prior to death.

Seisaku Nakamura

Hamamatsu Deaf Killer

The case of Seisaku Nakamura is one of the more unusual in the annals of serial murder. Nakamura was a Japanese national born in Hamamatsu, Shizuoka Prefecture, on the country's central-west coast in 1924. His early life, like that of many serial killers, was difficult. Seisaku was born deaf into a society that was less than sympathetic to such physical imperfections. His family, perhaps embarrassed by this disability, were hardly a buffer. He was frequently beaten, treated as an outcast and left on his own.

It has been noted that many serial killers who suffer such ostracism retreat into a fantasy world, fueled most often by revenge fantasies. This was certainly the case with Seisaku Nakamura. He developed a near obsession with the Samurai culture and enjoyed watching movies where Samurai slaughtered their victims with their lethal Katana swords.

Yet on the surface all appeared normal. Seisaku was a bright boy who excelled at school. He was polite and deferential. He endured his condition without complaint. He'd grown too, into a tall and strapping youth.

According to his own testimony, Nakamura committed his first murders on August 22, 1938, at the tender age of 14. The victims were two women who resisted him when he tried to rape them. These murders have never been verified and it is quite possible that they were hushed up by the authorities. Japan at the time was on a war footing, preparing for its conquest of the Pacific. The powers-that-be would not have wanted to sully the patriotic fervor with front page news of a brutal double murder.

Nakamura's next jaunt into sexual homicide however, was not as easy to ignore. It began on August 18, 1941, when a woman was found stabbed to death and another suffered severe injuries. Just two days later on August 20, three more people were found brutally slain, stabbed and hacked to death. The military authorities by now had a description of a young man seen walking casually away from the murder scenes but the information was suppressed for fear that it would cause panic among a populace already feeling the strains of war. As a result, Nakamura avoided capture. And he was about to kill again.

On September 27, Nakamura was at his parental home when he got into an argument with his brother. Matters quickly got heated and then turned violent, with Nakamura drawing a knife and plunging it into his sibling's chest, killing him instantly. He then turned the weapon on his terrified family, slashing and stabbing as they scurried for cover. Nakamura's father, sister, sister-in-law and young niece were all injured. Miraculously all of them survived their wounds. Questioned about the incident, the family refused to name their attacker. They were too afraid of retribution they said.

And that refusal would have tragic consequences for another family. On August 30, 1942, Nakamura spotted a young woman on the street and followed her home. Entering the residence, he dragged the woman to the ground and began ripping at her clothes. When the woman's husband tried to intercede, Nakamura drew a knife and slaughtered both parents before turning his weapon on the couple's terrified children. The younger boy and girl were stabbed and slashed to death before Nakamura turned his attention to the older girl. He tried to rape her but then suddenly broke off the attack and fled, leaving the girl alive.

The police meanwhile had been investigating the attack on the Nakamura family and had become convinced that the family was refusing to name their attacker because he was one of their own. Now with a description provided by the surviving victim of this latest atrocity, they honed in on their prime suspect Seisaku Nakamura.

Nakamura offered no resistance when he was arrested on October 12, 1942. And he made no attempt to deny that he was the man responsible for the killing spree which now included nine known victims. He described his crimes with relish, even adding the two murders he'd committed as a 14-year-old which the police had been unaware of. That brought his tally to eleven and he was about to indirectly claim a twelfth victim. Weighed down by the guilt and shame of his son's murderous rampage, Nakamura's father Fumisada took his own life.

Criminal justice is usually swiftly delivered in Japan and it was even more so during the war. Just 17 years of age at the time, Nakamura was deemed an adult and was tried as such. A procession of doctors was wheeled out during the trial to testify that Nakamura was insane and should be confined to a mental hospital. That testimony did him no good. Found guilty on nine counts of murder, the 'Hamamatsu Deaf Killer' was sentenced to death. He was executed by hanging on June 19, 1944.

Lam Kwok-wai

Sik Moh (Sex Devil)

Tuen Mun is a satellite town some two hours' drive from central Hong Kong. Built in the late 1970's to house manufacturing workers, it is a grim collective of crumbling concrete tower blocks, a place where juvenile crime and truancy are the highest in the region, where drugs are easily obtainable, where broken families, gambling addiction and unemployment are the norm. It is a world far removed from the glittering skyscrapers and plush hotels of downtown Hong Kong.

It was in Tuen Mun that Lam Kwok-wai was born in 1971 and here that he spent his formative years, crammed into a tiny 450-square-foot apartment with his father, stepmother and four siblings.

Life was difficult for the young Lam. His father, already 60 years old at the time of Lam's birth, was an alcoholic who ruled his brood with an iron fist. Nights were spent barricaded into the apartment watching TV in silence with his siblings while his father got slowly drunk on rice wine. The atmosphere was always tense. A careless word might earn a beating.

As time went by Lam became more and more withdrawn. He did poorly at school and eventually dropped out entirely at 15, having completed only Grade 7. That same year Lam's father got into trouble with a loan shark and had to flee to Macau. Seizing the opportunity at freedom, Lam began hanging with some local thugs, stealing, gambling and getting into street fights. He also began using drugs,

including Mandrax and marijuana. However none of them appealed to
him as much as alcohol.

Over time Lam gravitated towards a new form of excitement – illegal
street racing. He became a fearless racer, determined to win at all costs
even if it meant endangering his own life, those of fellow racers or of
pedestrians.

Then on April 24, 1992, Lam discovered a new kick that supplanted
even the thrill of racing. He'd been drinking heavily that day and into
the evening. Late at night he found himself sitting in a park when a
taxi stopped in front of Oi Ming House. An attractive young woman
got out and walked into the building and Lam followed, pushing his
way into the lift as the doors were closing. He immediately grabbed
the woman by the throat and strangled her into submission. She later
awoke on the third-floor staircase, her jeans around her ankles and
blood pooled on the ground.

The rape provoked very little reaction in Tuen Mun, where such
attacks are double the Hong Kong average.

Two months later Lam committed another rape, the victim a 32-year-
old woman who he attacked as she returned home from her job as a
waitress. Afterwards Lam went home, dropped onto his bunk bed fully
clothed and slept. None of his family bothered asking where he'd
been.

Keeping to this pattern, Lam waited two months before committing a
sexual assault on a 39-year-old woman, then two more months before
he raped a 32-year-old in a lift at Hing Ping House. One month later he

again employed his familiar M.O., bursting through the lift doors as they were about to close, grabbing the victim by the throat and throttling her into submission.

By now the press was no longer ignoring the Tuen Mun rapist. They dubbed him Sik Moh (Sex Devil) and speculated that it was only a matter of time before he killed someone.

So it proved. Three weeks after his last attack, Lam followed 50-year-old department store assistant Li Hing from a late night mahjong game. As always he confronted her in a lift, strangled her into unconsciousness and then dragged her into a stairwell. There he continued the attack, placing his hands on her throat and squeezing until she stopped breathing. He then raped and sodomized the corpse before walking away from the scene.

The rape and murder caused renewed panic in Tuen Mun, with local politicians slamming the police for their inept handling of the case while the community staged marches and demonstrations demanding better protection.

In response the police drafted in scores of undercover officers, including volunteer policewomen to act as bait for the killer rapist. A Midas computer system, similar to the one used in the Yorkshire Ripper case, was set up to keep track of the investigation. Everyone convicted of violence against women – be it wife battering, assault or sexual assault – was investigated. Lam, who had no such record, slipped through the net.

On April 14, 1993, Lam killed again. The victim was Mak Siu-han, a 22-year-old disc jockey at a local nightclub. She was found raped and strangled in a stairwell at Hing Shing House. Lam would later claim that he hadn't wanted to kill her but had squeezed her neck too hard.

The following night there were renewed demonstrations in Tuen Mun, with over 200 residents involved. Fearing that he might fall prey to the vigilante squads that were now prowling the streets, Lam fled Tuen Mun and went to stay with his elder sister in Hunghom. He'd been there only a few weeks when he murdered 23-year-old Lau Sui-man, a karaoke hostess.

On July 11, 1993, Lam committed another rape in Hunghom, although on this occasion he left his victim alive. Just short of a month later he struck again, in an attack that would lead to his undoing.

The victim was a 21-year-old woman who he dragged into an alley just off Mei King Street on August 8, 1993. He throttled, beat and kicked her, then threw her onto a wooden cart and began raping her. Then inexplicably he broke off the attack and started talking to the woman, chatting as though she were an old friend rather than someone he'd just brutalized and raped. Afraid of what he might do if she ignored him, she joined in the conversation, even sharing a cigarette with Lam before he walked her back to the road.

There he stopped and asked the petrified woman: "Will you be my girlfriend?" The woman said yes – anything to get away from him – and agreed to meet him at the Whampoa movie theater the next day. "Please be there," Lam implored her before he left.

The woman reported the incident to the police. However the task force was by now thinly spread and as investigators did not regard the lead as promising, they assigned only two undercover officers to stake out the movie theater. In order to bolster the numbers, the victim's brother went along.

At precisely 8.30 as arranged, Lam walked into the foyer of the theater. Spotting him the woman gave the prearranged signal to the surveillance team, scratching her hair. Nothing happened. She scratched again. Nothing. The cops had obviously been distracted. They probably believed that Lam was not stupid enough to walk into such an obvious trap.

Eventually, with Lam just feet away the woman started screaming, causing him to flee. The police officers gave chase but they got nowhere near him. The victim's brother went flying past and tackled Lam to the ground.

In custody Lam did his best to convince the police that he was insane. He cried, he screamed, he babbled. He went into convulsions and banged his head on the floor. He referred to his strangling hand as his "fork" and stared constantly at it, as though it were separate from his body. He spoke of seeing ghosts.

It was all to no avail. Lam was evaluated by psychiatrists and declared fit to stand trial. He was sentenced to life in prison. It is unlikely that he will ever be released.

Verry Idham Henyansyah

The Singing Serial Killer

On July 12, 2008, a delipidated suitcase and a couple of plastic bags were found on a street in Jakarta, Indonesia. The bags contained the dismembered remains of a middle-aged male, soon identified as 40-year-old businessman Heri Santoso. Having established the victim's identity, it took the Jakarta police only days to arrest a suspect, a young wannabe pop singer named Verry Idham Henyansyah, or as he preferred to be called, Ryan.

Ryan quickly confessed to the murder. In fact he didn't stop there, claiming he'd bludgeoned and stabbed 10 other people. Those bodies lay buried in the backyard of his parent's home in Jombang he said.

Verry Idham Henyansyah was born in Jombang, East Java on February 1, 1978. As a child he displayed a number of very worrying traits. He was prone to temper tantrums for one thing and quick to violence when things didn't go his way, attacking his parents and siblings with fists, nails and teeth. On other occasions he'd sit in a glowering silence, with everyone in the household afraid to approach him lest they set him off.

At school it was a different story, Ryan achieved good grades and was praised by his teachers for his exemplary behavior. He made few friends though and was often teased and taunted because of his "girly" looks. Nonetheless he graduated with honors and was accepted to study medicine at a local university, only to drop out because his parents couldn't afford the tuition fees.

Ryan began studying instead to become a Koran studies teacher. And it wasn't long before he was involved in a homosexual relationship with his instructor, an affair that would endure for nine years. When his lover eventually broke it off to enter into a heterosexual marriage, Ryan was devastated.

That devastation soon gave way to a glowering anger. Seeking an outlet he began cruising the local bars, picking up men. He'd bring them back to his room with the promise of sex. However the minute one of them made a move on him he'd explode and attack, bludgeoning and stabbing the man to death. He also on one occasion brought home a woman, Nanik Kristanti and her 3-year-old daughter Silvia, killing them in similar fashion. All of the bodies were buried in his backyard.

Ryan claims to remember very little about the murders although this is almost certainly a lie since he includes in his memoirs a detailed sketch showing exactly where each body is buried. What he does recall is his motivation for each killing and in true serial killer fashion, he is always ready to blame someone else.

"Most of the victims were gay men like me," he says. "They made me feel cheap. I got angry, we fought and I accidentally killed them.

"Zacky and Aksony (2 of the victims) did not only strike me with hurtful words, but their hands groped my vital organs (sex) so that I would date them. I hated their acts. Especially when my homosexuality was used as a reason for them to satiate their lust. Not all gay men are promiscuous. Love is very important to me. It makes me furious when people say there's no such thing as loyalty in the gay world."

As regards his female victims he said that Nanik tried to seduce him so he had to kill her. The little girl had to die because she witnessed her mother's murder.

With the disappearances of 10 people raising questions in his hometown, Ryan absconded next to Jakarta where he pursued a career as an aerobics instructor and part-time model, while also shopping his talents as a singer. He also found a new love. However that explosive temper of his soon led him into trouble.

When businessman Heri Santoso offered a car and cash if he could have sex with Ryan's boyfriend, Ryan was furious. On July 11, he invited Santoso to his rented house in the Margonda area of Depok. There he beat the man and sodomized him with a crowbar before hacking him to death with a knife. Eventually he cut Santoso's body into seven pieces, packed it in bags and dumped it on a street.

"I can't explain how it happened," he'd later claim. "I was furious and jealous. I only realized he was dead after I saw cut-up pieces of his flesh on my lap, the blood, the bad smell."

Verry Idham Henyansyah went on trial for murder in November 2008. Found guilty, he was sentenced to die by firing squad. He currently awaits execution at Kesambi Penitentiary in Cirebon.

However the case continues to be a sensation in Indonesia. Ryan has since released his memoirs as well as a pop album called "My Last Performance." Despite his homosexuality, he attracts scores of teenaged female fans who queue for hours at the prison in order to have their photos taken with him.

Surender Koli
& Moninder Singh Pandher

For two years residents of Nithari, on the outskirts of the Indian capital of New Delhi, had streamed to the local police station with complaints of missing children. Their complaints had been met with indifference, derision, even hostility. Not even the discovery of human bones or reports of a vile smell emanating from a drain in the area would spur the police into action.

On December 29, 2006, two men who had lost daughters eventually took their frustrations to Resident Welfare Association President S. C. Mishra. The men claimed that they knew the location of the remains of several missing children. They'd been disposed of in the drains behind the palatial home at number D5.

At first Mishra was skeptical. The house the men were referring to belonged to Moninder Singh Pandher, a millionaire businessman with political connections. Eventually though he was persuaded to join the two men in searching the drain. Almost immediately they discovered a decomposing hand. Within a short while three incomplete skeletons were recovered and the police were called.

As news of the discovery leaked out, anxious parents descended on the residence. Soon a full-scale riot was in progress, with police struggling to contain angry locals. As much for their own protection as for any other reason, Moninder Singh Pandher and his manservant Surender Koli were taken into custody. Soon Koli would begin talking, revealing one of the most horrendous cases of child serial murder in India's history.

Moninder Singh Pandher was born into a wealthy family in Punjab, graduating from Delhi's prestigious St. Stephen's College and inheriting a successful family business with interests in transport, real estate and agriculture. He grew up with a love of luxury, a taste for fine wine and single-malt whiskey, a fondness for golf and a yearning for international travel. In the years leading up to his arrest, he'd visited the United States, Switzerland, Dubai, Canada and China.

But not everything about Pandher's life was as idyllic as it seemed. He was estranged from his wife and lived apart from his family, barely seeing them. In lieu of familial companionship he spent his free time with prostitutes, usually procured by his servant Koli. As would later emerge, not all of his sexual partners were of age, or willing.

Surender Koli followed a quite different path to serial murder than his employer.

Born in Almora, Uttarakhand, Koli was a high school dropout who skinned animals for a living before abandoning his wife and child to move to Delhi. There he did various odd jobs as a cook and dishwasher before finding employment as a manservant to a retired army brigadier. The officer later introduced him to Moninder Singh Pandher. Not long after he left his employer to work for Pandher. Now both of them were in custody charged with murder.

While the search of the drain at Pandher's house continued to uncover more and more human remains, Pandher and Koli were sent to Gandhinagar for extensive narco-analysis. These procedures, involving polygraphs, truth serums and brain monitoring, are inadmissible in court. However, they are used to aid police in their investigation. In this case they produced some interesting results.

Only Koli was subjected to the truth serum, Pandher being excused on health grounds. Under its effects Koli provided contradictory statements. At first he said that Pandher was unaware of the killings and that he had committed the murders while Pandher was abroad.

Explaining his motive, Koli said that he had often acted as a procurer of prostitutes for his master and that seeing Pandher and his guests engaged in sexual acts with prostitutes had led to him becoming increasingly sexually frustrated. He also said that he was a necrophile and craved erotic contact with dead bodies.

His first victim was 14-year-old Rimpa Halder, who he strangled to death before having sex with her corpse. He then cut out the child's liver and tried to eat it but was immediately ill. Later he dismembered the body with a saw, dumped the larger pieces in the drain behind the house and flushed the innards and smaller pieces down the toilet.

So far Koli appeared to absolve Pandher of blame, but his later testimony contradicted this. He now said that after he lured a victim into the house with candy, he would rape the child before handing her over to Pandher. When Pandher was done sexually assaulting the victim, he (Koli) would strangle her, before dismembering the body and disposing of it.

He denied that the murders were part of an organ trafficking scam (as had at one time being suspected), although he confessed to cannibalizing the corpses. He also denied that the victims were used in child pornography, even though the police found nude pictures of Pandher with several children on his computer.

Pandher and Koli eventually went on trial in February 2009, by which time 38 victims (all but one aged between 3 and 11 years) had been identified from the remains pulled out of the drains at the Pandher residence. Both men were found guilty and both sentenced to death.

The case had far-reaching consequences, with an inquiry by the National Human Rights Commission that led to the dismissal of several police officers for dereliction of duty. In addition, the trial judge severely criticized India's CBI (Central Bureau of Investigation) who had taken over the case during its early stages. The CBI had sought to downplay Pandher's role in the murders, placing all of the blame on Koli.

Daisuke Mori

When you think about it, the role of medical caregiver is the perfect cover for a sociopathic killer. We trust them implicitly, literally with our lives. When they ask us to swallow a pill, we do so without hesitation. When they insert a needle into an arm we assume that whatever the syringe or catheter contains will do us good. This is not always the case.

Daisuke Mori worked at the 18-bed Hokuryo Clinic in Sendai, some 200 miles north of Tokyo, Japan. Not much about Daisuke stood out. He was a male nurse of some experience but average ability. The son of a police officer, he'd been a mediocre student but a talented athlete whose early promise had been curtailed by a ligament injury that two operations failed to correct. An introvert, he had few friends and no girlfriends during his school years.

After finishing high school, Mori decided to study for a nursing diploma. Having obtained that qualification he quickly found work at a local hospital, although his tenure there lasted just 18 months. This was to become a pattern with Mori. Over the next decade he worked at five different medical facilities, gaining a reputation as a hard worker with ambitions of advancement. The main reason that those aspirations weren't realized was down to Mori's frequent complaints about working conditions. Usually those complaints centered around pay and that is perhaps why he ended up at Hokuryo Clinic, a private hospice that paid above the going rate.

In 1999, Mori began dating a fellow nurse named Aiko, eight years his senior. Aiko was still married when they started seeing each other although she was estranged from her husband. Soon she and Mori had moved in together and in September 2000 she finally gained a divorce, leaving her free to remarry. By then Mori had already had a taste of domestic cohabitation and realized that it was not all wine and roses. He and Aiko fought frequently, often over trivialities. Mori, who at 29 had never been in a serious relationship before found this both perplexing and frustrating.

Was Daisuke Mori's domestic situation what eventually pushed him over the line to murder? We shall never know the answer for sure but it seems highly likely. Mori would certainly not be the first medical serial killer to follow this path. Nor is he likely to be the last. Frustrated by his frequent squabbles with Aiko and uncertain how to respond, Mori turned his ire on those closest to him – the patients under his care.

Mori's early victims were all elderly. A nursing home close to the Hokuryo Clinic routinely sent their residents there for check-ups or care. But from February 1999, a worrying trend began to emerge. During a 22-month period, five nursing home residents aged between 85 and 94 had been sent to the clinic for treatment, mainly of minor ailments. All had been attended by Daisuke Mori. All had died. Given the ages of the victims, the deaths drew minimal attention.

But Mori's victims were not confined entirely to the elderly. In September 2000, a toddler died soon after being given an injection by Mori. A month later an 11-year-old girl was admitted to the hospital complaining of stomach pains. A doctor diagnosed appendicitis and scheduled her for an appendectomy. But just 25 minutes later, after she was put on a drip by the attending nurse (Mori), her condition deteriorated rapidly and she started having difficulty breathing. Fortunately, in this case, doctors were able to intercede and save the girl's life but alarm bells were jangling. There was no logical explanation for the reaction the girl had shown. Unless that is, there was something in the drip that had affected her.

Dr. Ikuko Handa, vice director of the hospital, decided to investigate. He began questioning Mori's colleagues and soon had shocking anecdotal evidence. Mori it appeared had a nickname among his coworkers. They called him 'switcheroo Mori' because the minute he started taking care of a patient, the person's health appeared to take a rapid turn for the worse. This had been going on for over a year and yet no one had seen fit to inform the authorities.

Now though hospital administrators were spurred into action. They called the police and Mori was hauled in for questioning. Under interrogation he made no effort to deny the charges against him. Indeed he seemed perplexed that everyone was making such a fuss about it. Pressed for a motive, Mori insisted that he didn't have one. He bore no personal resentment towards the patients he said. He simply felt a compulsion to kill and acted on it.

The police were however able to learn more about Mori's method. He killed by introducing vecuronium bromide, a muscle relaxant used for general anesthesia, into his patients' drips. This powerful drug is often used to euthanize animals. It also has the ability to stop a human heart.

Miyagi Prefecture Police arrested and charged Mori on January 6, 2001. He would eventually be convicted on one count of murder and sentenced to life in prison. However the case had far broader implications than that. The administration of Japan's entire medical health system was dragged under the spotlight. What that spotlight revealed did little to reassure the nation.

Inadequate controls, both of health workers and of dangerous drugs, medical mistakes, negligence, mismanagement – all were rife. There was a widespread lack of transparency with patients prohibited from viewing their own medical charts. As a result, instances of malpractice went mostly unpunished and that in turn exacerbated the problem of lax controls. What incentive did hospitals have for putting in expensive monitoring systems when incidents of malpractice could be easily swept under the carpet? It all resulted in a vicious circle, with hospital patients bearing the brunt.

Yet even in the wake of the Mori case, the authorities were slow to implement changes, the powerful Japan Medical Association saw to that. It is only in recent years that there has been an increase in malpractice lawsuits in Japan. "Paternalism in medicine hasn't changed a bit," says Naoki Fukuchi, a lawyer who specializes in medical malpractice cases. "People have a fantasy that doctors are infallible. And doctors are eager to hide their mistakes."

Mistakes yes, and also their crimes. How long before another Daisuke Mori is uncovered in a Japanese hospital?

Chung Nam-gyu

Chung Nam-gyu had a grudge against the world, a hatred born of years on the fringes of society, unable to find a job and because of that, unable to marry and raise the family he longed for. At 35 the ex-convict was still living at home with his mother and siblings in the city of Incheon, near Seoul, South Korea. His life seemed pointless, without hope or prospects. His one pleasure he'd later tell investigators, was to ride the train from Incheon to Gangnam, where he'd walk the streets admiring the houses of the rich. More often than not though, he'd be stopped by a police cruiser and told to move along, which only served to fuel his resentment.

Chung had begun his criminal career in 1989, a year after he graduated high school. Like most young criminals he'd started with break-ins but unfortunately for him, he was not a particularly adept burglar. He soon found himself in custody, charged with "special robbery."

That earned him a two-and-a-half-year sentence. And he'd barely been released when he was arrested for breaking and entering and then for sexual assault. He'd be in and out of prison over the next two decades. Each arrest, each prison term, made him more and more resentful.

By 2004 Chung, who was still without a job and still living in poverty, began taking long nighttime walks around the city. At first these were to alleviate the frustration he felt brewing inside him but ever vigilant for the opportunity of an easy score, he began spying on homes and businesses, figuring out how he might break into them. He was acutely aware however that with his criminal record, his next prison term was likely to be a long one. If he was going back to prison he reasoned, it was going to be for something worthwhile.

At around this time Chung seems to have begun a personal boot camp. He took to working out every day, running ten kilometers and doing weight training to build up his strength. He began watching movies about serial killers like "The Silence of the Lambs," "Seven" and "Henry: Portrait of a Serial Killer." He started reading books on psychology, criminology and human biology. He also began secretly assembling a stash of weapons. Those who knew him had never seen Chung so motivated. Little did they know he was preparing for a murder spree.

According to Chung's later confession, his original idea was to target the rich. However, he knew from his walks around Gangnam that he had little chance of carrying out his campaign there. The area was dotted with surveillance cameras and patrolled by both police and private security firms. He'd be arrested before he even got started.

Reaching a compromise with himself, he directed his attention at the working class and middle-class suburbs of Geumcheon-gu, Gwanak-gu, Dongjak-gu and Yeongdeungpo-gu in southwestern Seoul.

From February 2004, the police began to notice a pattern of attacks in those areas. All of the victims were women living alone, bludgeoned or stabbed as they slept and then robbed of cash and valuables before the assailant fled, sometimes setting the home alight for good measure. Several of the assaults had been fatal.

One particularly callous attack occurred on March 27, 2004, at around 4:30 in the morning. On that occasion the killer broke into a second-floor apartment in Gwanak-gu. Finding three young girls asleep, he bludgeoned them with an iron bar, killing two and severely injuring the third. He then draped a blanket over the children and set it alight. The third victim later died from her injuries.

On April 18, 2004, he broke into a house in Geumcheon-gu, beat a 47-year-old woman and her 13-year-old son to death, then set the house on fire and fled with money and valuables. On October 9 that same year he entered a community center for the disabled in Bongcheon-dong and severely beat two mentally handicapped women with an iron bar.

By now a major operation was underway to catch the killer. But Chung's intimate knowledge of the suburbs, gained on his nighttime strolls, kept him one step ahead of the police. Then in April 2006 he made a mistake.

Chung had always been exceedingly careful in choosing his targets, preferring women living alone or with young children. At around 4:50 a.m. on Saturday, April 18, he made the error of entering a house in Yeongdeungpo-gu where a man was present. The homeowner Kim was already up, getting ready for an early shift. Finding Chung in his home, he beat him senseless and held him until the police arrived.

Chung Nam-gyu went on trial at the Seoul Southern District Court in September 2006, charged with 13 counts of murder and 20 of attempted murder. Found guilty of all charges he was sentenced to hang.

"I'm not sorry for the victims," he said in his final statement. "I feel proud to have killed such a large number of people."

Chung was sent to the Seoul Detention House in Uiwang to await execution. However despite retaining the death penalty statute, South Korea had not actually executed anyone in over 10 years. Fierce debate was raging at the time regarding the legitimacy of "state-sanctioned homicide" and there is every chance that Chung's sentence would eventually be commuted to life in prison.

In the end Chung took that decision out of the hands of the lawmakers. He hung himself in his cell on November 22, 2009.

Li Wenxian

The Guangzhou Ripper

Before the fall of the Berlin Wall and the subsequent adoption of capitalism in Russia and China, communist societies did not acknowledge the presence of serial killers. Such creatures were a product of western decadence they said, they did not exist in a "workers' paradise."

This of course was pure propaganda, an ill-advised stance that allowed such monsters to prosper. Men like Andrei Chikatilo, who claimed 55 lives across the Soviet Union, or the Ukrainian psycho Anatoly Onoprienko, slayer of at least 52 people. Neither was China immune from the plague of serial killers, as witnessed by the infamous cases of the "Cannibal Monster" Zhang Yongming and the "Red Dress Killer" Duan Guocheng. Both of these psychopaths however were preceded by Li Wenxian, a fearsome serial killer who went by the nickname "The Guangzhou Ripper."

The ripper first surfaced in early 1991, when on February 22, he slashed and stabbed a 20-year-old woman to death and then inflicted horrific postmortem wounds on her corpse. The police had barely launched their investigation into that slaying when another brutalized body turned up, then another.

Over the next six months a total of five young women were brutally slain. All had been the victim of a sexual assault and had then been strangled or stabbed to death. Afterwards the killer hacked their bodies apart, stuffed the segments into rice bags and discarded them at the numerous informal rubbish dumps that dotted the squalid suburbs around Guangzhou.

The investigation into the murders was particularly inept, with senior officers more concerned with keeping the murders under wraps than hunting down the killer. There was also no coverage of the crimes in the tightly controlled state media, leaving the bulk of the populace blissfully unaware of the monster in their midst. When the murders suddenly stopped the authorities breathed a collective sigh of relief. The nightmare was over and although their quarry had escaped justice, at least his presence had remained a secret to all but a few.

But the ripper hadn't gone away. After laying fallow for half a year, he struck again and this time the Chinese were powerless to keep the details out of the press as the mutilated corpse washed up in Hong Kong, still under British rule at that time.

The following day the South China Morning Post carried a front-page article about the gruesome discovery. According to the report the young female victim had been slit open from throat to gut and then crudely stitched up again. All of her fingers had also been severed, possibly in an effort to prevent identification. At any rate, no person matching the victim's description had been reported missing from Hong Kong and it was therefore assumed that the corpse was from mainland China.

With the eyes of the world now firmly focused on China, the government was belatedly spurred into action, handing responsibility for the case to the head of Guangzhou's Criminal Investigation Department, Zhu Minjian. He responded in predictable fashion, reporting via the official news channels that if a serial killer was operating in Guangzhou, he was likely a dissident who had copied such methods from western murderers. He would nonetheless be brought swiftly to justice, Zhu Minjian assured the Chinese people.

That promise would prove to be naively optimistic. Over the next four years the Guangzhou Ripper remained at large, claiming the lives of at least seven more women. He also added a new method of mayhem to his armory. Later victims had their skulls shattered by vicious blows from a claw hammer.

But the clock was ticking on the ripper's murderous career. Serial killers are often caught when they veer from their tried and tested M.O. and so it proved with the ripper. In November 1996, he attacked his fourteenth known victim, bludgeoning her into submission with a hammer, raping her and leaving her for dead. The woman though would survive her horrendous injuries and later identify her attacker. He was Li Wenxian, a former farmer from southern Guangdong province who had moved to Guangzhou in 1991. He'd been working since then as a laborer.

Wenxian was quickly tracked down and taken into custody, where a few hours of police "persuasion" convinced him to confess. He said that he'd committed the murders to exact revenge on women after he'd been cheated by a prostitute.

Li Wenxian went on trial before the Intermediate People's Court in December 1996. Convicted on several charges of murder, rape and robbery, he was sentenced to death. Details of his execution were not released, although he is believed to have been put to death in early 1997.

Charles Sobhraj

The Serpent

Conman, jewel thief, drug dealer and murderer, Charles Sobhraj is likely the most unusual serial killer you will ever read about. This incredibly audacious psychopath pulled off innumerable criminal scams stretching from Europe across the Middle East and into Asia. He escaped from several of the world's toughest prisons and even retired to live a near celebrity lifestyle. Lest we forget, he also murdered at least 12 people.

Charles Sobhraj was born on April 6, 1944, in Saigon, Vietnam. His father was an Indian tailor, his mother a Vietnamese peasant. Shortly after Charles' birth his father abandoned the family. His mother later married a French soldier and moved to Marseilles, taking Charles with her.

Charles was unhappy in France and stowed away several times on ships bound for the Far East, on one occasion even making it all the way to be reunited with his father. He was promptly sent back to

France, where he grew from a difficult child into a rebellious teenager who despite his obvious intellect did poorly in school and often played truant.

During his early teens, Charles became a prodigious shoplifter and petty thief. Inevitably this led to more serious crimes and a burglary arrest in Paris eventually saw him sentenced to three years at the tough Poissy Prison.

A slightly built Asian teenager should have been easy meat for the prison predators but Charles was adept at using both his fists and his charm. The former helped him ward off sexual advances, the latter got him into the good graces of prison warders and gained him privileges and leniency.

His engaging nature also won him the friendship of a volunteer worker at the prison, a wealthy young man named Felix d'Escogne. Upon his release from Poissy, Sobhraj was invited to stay with d'Escogne and through this contact he was soon hobnobbing with some of the best families in Paris. Little did they know that the charming young man Felix introduced to them was simultaneously involved in all manner of criminal activity.

Shortly after moving in with Felix, Sobhraj met the woman who would become his wife. Chantal was from a good family and her parents were strongly opposed to the union. Nonetheless the young woman was smitten and after Sobhraj completed his latest period of incarceration, the couple was married. Just months after the nuptials, Sobhraj fled Paris in the middle of the night with a pregnant Chantal in tow and the gendarmes in hot pursuit.

They drove east in a car that Sobhraj had stolen from his friend Felix, crossing eastern Europe and the Middle East. Eventually, leaving a trail of bad checks and conned tourists in their wake, they reached Bombay, where Chantal gave birth to a baby girl.

Charles and Chantal integrated easily into expatriate French society and Charles soon set himself up in business, smuggling stolen luxury cars over the border from Pakistan and selling them at a handsome profit. He also financed a number of criminal gangs in carrying out various jewel thefts.

The Sobhrajs were doing well. But unfortunately most of Charles' ill-gotten gains went straight to feeding his gambling addiction. By 1971 he was in deep hock to a number of Macau casino owners who were beginning to ask (none too politely) after their money.

Then came an opportunity to wipe off his debt in one fell swoop. Sobhraj was hired to carry out a jewelry heist at the luxury Ashoka Hotel in Delhi. He duly kidnapped the store owner and forced him to hand over $10,000 in cash and an even greater value in gems. The man was then tied up as the thieves fled. Unfortunately for Sobhraj, he got loose and raised the alarm.

Forced to dump the loot in order to make his escape, Sobhraj was captured on his return to Bombay and was sent to the notorious Tihar prison. He escaped soon after by feigning illness. He then fled with his family to Kabul, Afghanistan.

Over the next few years Sobhraj traveled around Europe and the Middle East, staying in Karachi, Rome, Teheran, Kabul, Copenhagen, Zagreb and Sofia.

He used various aliases and although he continued to support himself through criminal schemes, he never stopped long enough in one place to arouse suspicion. Eventually he abandoned his family in Kabul and Chantal returned to Paris, never to see Charles Sobhraj again.

Soon Sobhraj had a new accomplice, his younger half-brother Andre. The two took to robbing tourists in Greece and Turkey. When they were captured Sobhraj again managed to escape, leaving his sibling to face 18 years in a Turkish prison.

Sobhraj showed up next in India, then in Iran, duping and robbing French and English-speaking tourists. While running these scams he met a woman who would become his lover and long-time accomplice, a French Canadian named Marie LeClerc.

Together with Marie, Sobhraj moved to Bangkok where his criminal career entered a whole new chapter. Sobhraj had long dreamt of assembling a criminal cult along the lines of the Manson family. Now he began assembling his team, first duping a French boy named Dominique and then two ex-policemen named Yannick and Jacques into joining him. The final member of the team was a sociopathic young Indian named Ajay Chowdhury, who became Sobhraj's right-hand man.

It is uncertain whether Sobhraj had murdered anyone up to this point, but that was soon to change.

His first victim was an American named Jennie Bollivar, who fell in with the Sobhraj gang for a while before ending up dead in a tidal pool in the Gulf of Thailand. At first it was thought that the young woman had drowned accidently, but an autopsy later showed that someone had held her head under water.

The next to die was a young man named Vitali Hakim. Like Jennie Bollivar, he stayed with Sobhraj and his crew for a couple of days before disappearing while on a trip to the Gulf of Thailand with Sobhraj and Chowdhury. His badly burned body was found several days later on the road to Pattaya. It was determined that he'd still been alive when set alight. The police blamed Thai bandits.

In December 1975, Vitali Hakim's girlfriend, a French citizen named Charmayne Carrou, came looking for him. Within days she was dead, the circumstances of her death almost identical to Jennie Bollivar. An autopsy would later prove that she hadn't drowned, she'd been strangled.

Henk Bintanja and his fiancée Cornelia Hemker were Dutch students traveling around Southeast Asia when they met Charles Sobhraj in Hong Kong. He invited them to stay at his house in Bangkok and they were happy to take him up on his offer. Sobhraj's initial plan was to dupe the couple out of their valuables. But when Charmayne Carrou showed up making accusations about the missing Vitali Hakim, he panicked.

The day after Charmayne died, Henk and Cornelia left with Sobhraj and Chowdhury and never returned. The following day the Bangkok papers reported that two tourists had been murdered by bandits. They had been strangled before being set alight.

On December 18, the day the bodies of Bintanja and Hemker were identified, Sobhraj and LeClerc entered Nepal using the couple's passports. There they met and befriended Canadian Laurent Ormond Carriere, 26, and Californian Connie Bronzich, 29 years old. Just days later the bodies of Carriere and Bronzich were found in a field. They'd both been stabbed to death and then set alight.

A short while later, Sobhraj flew out of Nepal and re-entered Thailand on Carriere's passport.

Sobhraj was in for a surprise when he got home. While he'd been away, Dominique, Yannick and Jacques had broken into his office and discovered the passports and identity papers of dozens of tourists who'd either been duped or killed by Sobhraj. The three had fled the country but before leaving, they'd clued the authorities in about Sobhraj's criminal activities.

With the Thai authorities after him, Sobhraj headed back to India where he murdered Israeli scholar Avoni Jacob and stole his passport and traveler's checks. He then flew back to Thailand using Jacob's passport.

Not long after his return to Bangkok, Sobhraj was pulled in for questioning regarding the deaths of Jennie Bollivar and Charmayne Carrou. But the interrogation was half-hearted, the questions at best cursory. Sobhraj was released after just a few hours.

He flew immediately to Malaysia with Marie LeClerc and Ajay Chowdhury in tow. Shortly after their arrival Chowdhury disappeared, never to be seen again. It appears that he'd outlived his usefulness to Sobhraj.

But by now time was running out for Charles Sobhraj. The Thai authorities, who had thus far been particularly lax in investigating his activities, were disturbed by stories of a serial killer targeting tourists. Thailand's economy relies heavily on tourism and murdered travelers could only hurt that trade.

Additionally the American, Canadian, French and Dutch embassies were asking questions about their murdered citizens. Interpol was also on the case and had been tracking Sobhraj since the Ashoka Hotel heist. And a Dutch embassy employee named Herman Knippenberg was building a case against Sobhraj for the murders of Henk Bintanja and Cornelia Hemker. Knippenberg would continue compiling his dossier over the years, something that would eventually come back to haunt Sobhraj.

So where was the fugitive?

He was back in Bombay with Marie LeClerc, working his old scams again. He'd also managed to recruit two new western women to his cause, Barbara Sheryl Smith and Mary Ellen Eather.

The first crime that he pulled off with this new team went horribly wrong. The mark, a Frenchman named Jean-Luc Solomon, was drugged with the intent of robbing him. Unfortunately, Sobhraj miscalculated the dosage and the man died without regaining consciousness.

Unperturbed by this failure, Sobhraj tried an even more audacious scheme. Offering himself as a tour guide to a group of 60 French students, he handed out pills for them to take, telling them that the medication would prevent dysentery.

The plan was to drug the students and then rob their hotel rooms but again the dosage was too potent. When the students began collapsing in the hotel lobby, Sobhraj and his gang were apprehended and the police were called.

Barbara and Mary Ellen quickly cracked and told everything. In short order and despite his protestations of innocence, Sobhraj was charged with murdering Jean-Luc Solomon and sent to Tihar Prison, where he'd been held years before.

Not that he was particularly concerned. He'd managed to smuggle in 70 carats worth of gems and was soon greasing palms and being treated like royalty. His co-defendants meanwhile were living in such appalling conditions that both Barbara and Mary Ellen attempted suicide.

Eventually Sobhraj went on trial. It was widely expected that he'd be sentenced to death but when the verdict came down it was extremely lenient, seven years for involuntary homicide plus five for poisoning the French students.

Sobhraj was unconcerned by the sentence. In fact, he would have preferred a longer term. There was still an outstanding murder warrant from Thailand which would remain valid for 20 years. He knew that he was likely to be executed if handed over to the Thai authorities.

So he was happy to bide his time. Why wouldn't he be? As the years rolled by he virtually ran the Tihar prison. No luxury was denied him and he could even come and go as he pleased. As his ten-year anniversary rolled around he staged an escape, allowing himself to be recaptured a few days later. The aim wasn't to flee he later admitted, but to add a few years to his sentence while the Thai warrant expired.

On February 17, 1997, Sobhraj walked out of Tihar Prison a free man. He   returned to France where he became an instant celebrity. A movie company was reported to have paid him $15 million for the rights to a film about his life, while journalists queued to interview him at $5,000 a time. It seemed that, despite the old adage, crime did pay.

But if anyone in this world was due a healthy serving of bad karma, it was Charles Sobhraj. And so it proved.

In September 2003, for motives unknown Sobhraj traveled to Nepal, a country that still had two outstanding murder warrants out for him. Spotted on the streets of Kathmandu, he was quickly arrested.

On August 20, 2004, the Kathmandu District Court sentenced Charles Sobhraj to life imprisonment for the murders of Laurent Carriere and Connie Bronzich. Much of the evidence against him came from the painstaking work of Herman Knippenberg, the Dutch official who had been so determined to bring him to justice.

Futoshi Matsunaga

Japan has produced fewer serial killers than most major industrialized nations. However, some of those that it has produced are among the most depraved in the annals of criminal history. Like Sataro Fukiage, rapist and killer of at least seven juvenile girls during the 1920's, or Yoshio Kodaira, a necrophile who left behind a trail of ravished corpses in Tokyo during World War II. Then there's Seito Sakakibara. Just 14 years old, he attacked four younger children with a hammer, killing and then beheading two of them. None of these miscreants though, compares to Futoshi Matsunaga, a man whose crimes were so atrocious that the Japanese media withheld many of the details from the public.

Futoshi Matsunaga was born on April 28, 1961, in Kokura Kita-ku, Japan. Shortly after his birth his family moved to Yanagawa, where he grew up and attended school. Matsunaga was a good student who was well-liked by his peers and teachers. However from an early age he showed signs of rebelliousness as well as a precocious interest in sex. Eventually it got him into trouble when he was expelled for carrying on a relationship with a much younger girl.

Despite this setback, Matsunaga moved to another school and managed to graduate. By 19 he was married, a union that would last seven years and produce a son, despite Matsunaga's ill treatment of his wife and his openly flaunted affairs.

In October 1982, while still married, Matsunaga met an impressionable young girl named Junko Ogata. Junko was instantly besotted with the smooth talking Matsunaga, who promised to marry her as soon as he could arrange a divorce from his wife. Junko's mother Shizumi did not approve of the relationship and encouraged her daughter to break it off. When Matsunaga got to hear of it he visited Shizumi, beat and raped her and then promised worse if she interfered again.

Matsunaga had by now gained complete control over Junko, manipulating her through physical and psychological abuse, threats of violence and declarations of love. Driven to the depths of despair by his unending cruelty, Junko attempted suicide in February 1985. Ever the opportunist, Matsunaga seized on the unfortunate woman's turmoil. He convinced Junko that her family no longer wanted anything to do with her and encouraged her to move in with him, thus cutting off her last familial ties. From that point on Junko was effectively his slave.

At around that time Matsunaga was running a futon company, using it as a front for his fraudulent activities. One such scam in 1992 netted him 180 million yen (about $2.2 million). When the victims went to the police Matsunaga dropped out of sight, taking Junko with him. They would remain fugitives for the next six years.

But even with the police hunting him and enough money to keep a low profile, Matsunaga could not quell his criminal nature. In April 1993 he seduced a wealthy married woman and convinced her to leave her husband. The woman and her three children moved in with Matsunaga and Junko (who Matsunaga claimed was his sister). He then systematically began defrauding the woman, eventually netting over 11.8 million yen ($145,000). When there was no more money to be gained from her, the woman and one of her children disappeared. Their bodies have never been found.

In 1994 Matsunaga and Junko were living in a condominium in Kokura Kita-ku when he found a new victim. One of Matsunaga's neighbors Kumio Toraya made the grave mistake of confiding in Matsunaga some information about his criminal past. Matsunaga immediately started blackmailing him. Then when he feared that the man might leave to escape his influence, he took Kumio and his daughter hostage, holding them in his apartment.

Over the next two years Matsunaga tortured Kumio with electric shocks, made him eat his own feces and forced him and his 9-year-old daughter to attack and beat each other. He kept them in a freezing bathroom during the height of winter without blankets and would often spray them with icy water.

When Kumio died on February 26, 1996, Matsunaga forced his daughter to eat a broth that he said had been cooked from her father's flesh. He then convinced the girl that she was responsible for her father's death and coerced her into chopping up his body and driving to the Kunisaki Peninsula with Junko to throw the remains into the sea.

Matsunaga's next victim was an acquaintance of Kumio's who arrived to enquire about his whereabouts and soon fell for Matsunaga's well-honed charms. Following a well-trodden path he seduced the woman, promised to marry her and then began relieving her of her savings. When the woman eventually got wind of what was happening, he took her and her daughter captive, holding them for several months before the woman managed to escape by jumping from a second-floor window. The woman went to the police but by the time they arrived Matsunaga and Junko were long gone. Traumatized by her ordeal, the woman would later be committed to a mental hospital.

Perhaps emboldened by the escape of their captive, Junko attempted an escape of her own in April 1997. When Matsunaga found out she was missing, he contacted Junko's family and threatened to expose Junko as a murderer unless they told him her whereabouts. The girl then meekly returned, but Matsunaga wanted more now.

First he extorted 63 million yen from Junko's family. Then he coerced Junko's married sister Rieko into submitting to his sexual demands. Eventually he took the family hostage and began to inflict abuse and torture upon them. Junko's mother Shizumi and her sister Rieko were tortured with electric shocks to their genitals. Junko's 61-year-old father Takashige was also electrocuted, eventually dying from his injuries on December 21, 1997.

After her husband's death, Shizumi's mental state began to deteriorate rapidly. On January 20, 1998, Matsunaga ordered Rieko and her husband Kazuya to strangle Shizumi. Under threat of torture and death, they complied.

The next to die was Rieko herself, strangled to death by her husband while the couple's 10-year-old daughter Aya held her down and Matsunaga hovered nearby with his electrical cables lest they waver. After Rieko's death Matsunaga confined Kazuya to a bathroom, where he died of starvation on April 13, 1998.

Matsunaga's next crime was his most depraved yet. On May 17, 1998, he forced 10-year-old Aya to strangle her 5-year-old brother Yuki while Junko and Kumio's daughter held the boy down. Three weeks later on June 7, 1998, he had Kumio's daughter kill Aya by strangulation.

With all of his captives now disposed of, Matsunaga again turned his attentions outward, seducing another woman in 2000 and defrauding her of 20 million yen. Fortunately for the woman, she never acceded to his suggestion that she move in.

By 2002, Kumio's daughter had been Matsunaga's prisoner for eight years. The girl was now 17 years old and with Aya's murder to hold over her, Matsunaga must have believed he had her under complete control. He began to grant her more latitude and on March 6, 2002, she escaped and went directly to the police. Matsunaga and Junko were arrested the following day.

Once in custody, Matsunaga tried to talk himself out of trouble by deflecting all of the blame onto Junko. Kumio's daughter soon put paid to that but while Junko was absolved of being the dominant partner, the girl's testimony indicated that she was far from passive and was a willing participant in the murders.

The pair were charged with seven murders, found guilty on six and sentenced to death. Junko's sentence was later reduced on appeal to life imprisonment but there was no such concession for Futoshi Matsunaga. He currently awaits execution.

Ahmad Suradji

Indonesia is a country of contrasts. On the one hand you have a burgeoning, developing nation, typified by the skyscrapers of its capital city Jakarta. On the other you have a country where old beliefs and superstitions persist, the reliance on witchdoctors for example. Such mystic advisors are commonplace in Indonesia and make a good living providing advice on matters such as money, romance and health. And their clientele is by no means restricted to uneducated country bumpkins. Go to any shopping mall in urban Indonesia and you're likely to find a stall set up by at least one of these practitioners, doing a swift and profitable trade.

One man who made his living in this way was Ahmad Suradji, a respected sorcerer living in Medan, the capital of the North Sumatra province. Many relied on his advice and his business flourished, so much so that he was able to buy a farm and become a cattle breeder. Like many in his profession, Ahmad was always looking for ways to increase his mystic powers. And one night he had a dream that showed him how he could do exactly that.

In the dream Ahmad was visited by his long dead father. The senior man told him that in order to access a greater source of supernatural power, he'd have to kill 70 women and drink their saliva. Ahmad took the apparition at its word.

At the time many of Ahmad Suradji's clients were women, either prostitutes seeking to make themselves more attractive to men or ordinary women wanting him to cast spells that would make their husbands or lovers faithful. This was of course very convenient for the soon-to-be serial killer. He didn't have to go looking for victims, they came looking for him. Not only that but they willingly participated in their own deaths, only realizing what Ahmad had in mind when it was too late.

Over the next decade from 1986 to 1997, Ahmed committed at least 42 murders. His modus operandi seldom varied. He'd arrange for a client to meet him at his farm where he'd convince her to walk with him into the sugarcane fields. There he'd have a pre-prepared hole dug and he'd ask the victim to step into it. He'd then bury her up to the waist. Don't worry he'd say, this is all part of the ritual. However once the woman was incapacitated, he'd loop a rope around her neck and strangle her to death. He'd then lick the saliva that had dribbled from her mouth during her death throes.

Suradji would then remove the body and bury it elsewhere on the farm, always close to his house with the head facing towards his homestead. This he believed would also increase his magical powers.

It seems incredible that 42 women could vanish after going to see Suradji and that no suspicion was attached to him. However, in this Suradji was helped by the victims themselves. The police were not going to put in any great effort to find missing prostitutes. And as for the other women, most of them were embarrassed by the purpose of their visit to the witchdoctor and therefore kept it a secret from friends and family.

But Suradji was never going to get away with wholesale slaughter indefinitely. Eventually the father of one of the missing women went to the police and voiced his suspicions about what had happened to her. Police officers then called on Suradji's farm and carried out a search, uncovering a recently buried corpse. A more thorough search of the property yielded 41 more bodies, many of them mere skeletal remains.

Ahmad Suradji was arrested on May 2, 1997, along with his three wives. In custody he confessed to murdering 42 women and girls ranging in age from 11 to 30 years. He seemed genuinely to believe that his motive justified the killings. He'd be proven wrong in that assumption. Both Suradji and his senior wife Tumini were charged with murder.

By the time the matter came to trial in April 1998, Suradji had changed his story. He now claimed that he'd killed no one and knew nothing about the bodies buried on his farm. His confession he said, had been beaten out of him by the police.

But Suradji's mystical powers should have told him that such a defense was never going to hold up, especially as the victims' clothing and personal effects had been found in his house.

Ahmad Suradji was found guilty of murder on April 27, 1998. The sentence of the court was that he be put to death by firing squad. That sentence was eventually carried out on July 10, 2008.

Yoshio Kodaira

Yoshio Kodaira is Japan's most prolific serial killer. The son of a violent alcoholic, Kodaira suffered severe beatings in childhood, leaving him with a stutter and with learning disabilities. He was also described by his elementary school teachers as "inattentive and listless" with a quick temper that saw him involved in fights just about every day.

Despite these difficulties Kodaira did eventually graduate, finishing 21st in a class of 23 students. Shortly thereafter he began an apprenticeship as a metalworker but in common with most serial killers, he was unable to hold down a job for very long. At 18 he fathered a son. Unprepared to take up the responsibility of parenthood, he refused to marry the child's mother. Soon after he joined the Imperial Japanese Navy in order to escape his parental obligations.

Kodaira disliked military discipline. But life in the military brought other compensations, like the prostitutes he visited in various ports of call.

In 1927 Kodaira was involved in Japanese military action against China, including the Jinan Incident when he killed six Chinese soldiers. He was also an active and willing participant in atrocities against Chinese civilians, describing one incident thus:

"Four or five of my comrades and I entered a Chinese home, tied up the father and locked him in the closet. We stole their jewelry and raped the women. We even bayoneted a pregnant woman and pulled out the fetus from her stomach. I also engaged in those depraved actions."

By 1932 Kodaira had completed his tour of duty in the navy. That same year he married the daughter of a Shinto priest. Her father objected to the union and he was soon proved right when Kodaira's wife left him after he impregnated another woman. On June 2, 1932, Kodaira arrived at the home of his in-laws and demanded that his wife return to him. When she refused he responded in typical fashion, attacking her family with an iron bar, beating her father to death and severely injuring six other family members.

That earned him 15 years at hard labor, but he served less than eight before being released under the terms of the general amnesty of 1940.

Free again, Kodaira found work as a civilian employee at a naval base in Tokyo. With a war on, most of his colleagues were young women and Kodaira soon figured out a way to spy on them as they showered after work. On May 25, 1945, he took things one step further. Finding 19-year-old Miyazaki Mitsuko alone in the bathroom, he raped and strangled her and then hid her corpse behind an air raid shelter.

With a war-torn Japan in chaos and on the brink of collapse, the crime went undiscovered and uninvestigated. Emboldened by the lack of police action, Kodaira killed again on June 22, this time raping and strangling 30-year-old Ishikawa Yori.

Kodaira had by now acquired a taste for murder. On July 12 he struck again, brutalizing and killing 32-year-old Nakamura Mitsuko. Just three days later on July 15 he claimed a fourth victim, 22-year-old Kondo Kazuko. Matsushita Yosh'e, 21, died on September 28, 17-year-old Shinokawa Tatsue on October 31. On December 30 Kodaira killed his eighth victim, 19-year-old Baba Hiroko.

By now the war had ended but the turmoil left behind in a defeated Japan provided the ideal conditions for a predator like Kodaira. He adjusted his M.O., loitering in public spaces and approaching young women with offers of food and other necessities. The first victim caught by this ruse was 15-year-old Abe Yoshiko, slain on June 30, 1946.

On July 10 Kodaira struck up a conversation with 17-year-old Midorikawa Ryuko. The initial discourse centered on the possibility of buying black market goods but Kodaira found that he actually liked the young woman. When she invited him for a meal he readily agreed, even meeting her parents and (foolishly as it turned out) giving them his real name.

Ryuko disappeared on August 6 after leaving home to meet with Kodaira. Her nude corpse was found at Zoioji Temple a few days later beside a second body, that of 16-year-old Shinokawa Tatsue.

Kodaira was the obvious suspect and after getting his name from Midorikawa Ryuko's parents, it did not take long for the police to track him down. He made no pretense at innocence, freely confessing to 10 murders and over 30 counts of rape. Brought to trial in August 1947, he was sentenced to death, that sentence carried out at Miyagi Prison on the morning of October 5, 1949.

Gholomreza Kordiyeh
The Tehran Vampire

Serial killers are an uncommon, though not unheard of, phenomenon in the strict Islamic Republic of Iran, a point amply illustrated by the high-profile cases of Mohammed Bijeh and Saeed Hanai. Another Iranian serial killer of recent vintage is Gholomreza Kordiyeh, a heartless psychopath who claimed the lives of nine women and young girls during a five-month killing spree in 1997.

Kordiyeh first attracted the attention of the police in 1993 when, at age 24, he was arrested for kidnapping and rape. He'd never stand trial on those charges however. On the way to the courthouse he managed to overpower his guard and escape. He would remain at large for four years. By the time he was eventually dragged before a judge, the charges would be much more serious.

No one knows where Kordiyeh hid out during his years on the run, nor what crimes he committed. What we do know is that he re-emerged in Teheran in February 1997 to snuff out the lives of eight women and a 10-year-old girl.

Kordiyeh's M.O. involved a simple yet highly effective ploy. He'd cruise the streets of Teheran by night posing as a cab driver. Once a female victim entered his car he'd engage the child lock, preventing her from opening the door. Then he'd drive to an isolated spot where he'd rape the woman repeatedly before dispatching her in a frenzied knife attack.

In an effort to conceal forensic evidence he'd then bundle the body out of the car, soak it with gasoline and light it on fire. Usually the corpse would be burned beyond recognition but in some instances, the flames died out before doing their job. In these cases, autopsies would reveal the ferocity of the killer. Several of the bodies bore more than 30 stab and slash wounds.

As the brutalized corpses continued to pile up, the police launched a desperate hunt for the so-called "Teheran Vampire." But they had no inkling of the crafty disguise Kordiyeh was using. As a taxi driver he was free to cruise the streets without attracting attention, free to pick up unsuspecting victims who got willingly into his cab. Who knows how long he might have continued had he not gotten careless and allowed two of his intended victims to escape.

The women went to the police and reported that they had been attacked by a cab driver. They then assisted a sketch artist in drawing up an identikit. Armed with this information, the police launched a massive stop-and-search operation in the Iranian capital. Hundreds of cabbies were pulled over. One of them, Gholomreza Kordiyeh, was taken into custody when it was found that he did not possess the required paperwork to operate a cab. Under interrogation he soon broke down and admitted that he was the elusive 'Vampire.'

Kordiyeh was swiftly put on trial, with the case attracting such massive interest that the Justice Department acceded to requests and allowed the proceedings to be broadcast live on state-run television. The evidence against the accused, which included forensics and eyewitness testimony (not to mention his own confession) was overwhelming. It came as no surprise that the verdict was guilty, or that the sentence was death by hanging.

Gholomreza Kordiyeh was publically executed on August 12, 1997, before a chanting crowd of over 20,000 spectators held back by razor wire and with over 1,000 riot policemen in place to keep the peace. In keeping with Islamic law, Kordiyeh was first subjected to 214 lashes, the blows delivered by relatives of his victims. Then a rope was fixed around his neck and he was hoisted into the air by a construction crane. For a brief moment his legs kicked out in erratic movements and then he was still.

But if the Iranian authorities thought that the public execution would serve as a deterrent to other would-be killers, they were to receive a rude wake-up call. Before the year was out, police arrested another cabbie after an assault on a female passenger. Under interrogation he apparently boasted that he was going to be the next "Teheran Vampire."

Yang Xinhai

The Monster Killer

China has produced a number of horrendous serial killers over the past few decades. None however is as prolific as Yang Xinhai, a demented psychopath who annihilated 67 victims over a four-year killing spree, hacking and bludgeoning them with hammers, meat cleavers, axes, shovels, anything he could lay his hands on.

Yang Xinhai was born on July 17, 1968. As a boy he was described as sensitive and intelligent, with a love of books. This went beyond reading. Yang also authored his own stories, filling every exercise book and scrap of paper with his meanderings, although he would allow no one to read them. When a relative sneaked a peak at the stories the boy was creating, he was shocked at its content. Yang had invented a fictional place that he called "Plato Heights," using it as a setting for stories of murder, mutilation and mayhem.

There were other signs too that all was not right with Yang. He was prone to rambling to himself and to flying off the handle at the slightest provocation. A promising student when he was younger, Yang lost interest in his studies once he entered high school, eventually dropping out in 1985 and finding work as a laborer.

Out on his own Yang hit the road, traveling between towns on foot or by bicycle, stopping wherever he found work and moving on whenever the mood took him. He also fell into a life of crime, graduating from petty theft to burglary to rape. Inevitably the law caught up with him. He was sent to "Re-education Through Labor" camps on two occasions, in 1988 and 1991. Then in 1996 he earned a five-year prison term for a rape committed in Zhumadian, Henan Province.

Yang emerged from prison in 2000 with a deep sense of injustice and a seething hatred against society. However, his anger was assuaged somewhat when he met a young woman and fell in love. The young lady appeared equally smitten at first but when she found out that Yang had served prison time for rape, she dumped him. It was the tipping point, the spark that ignited Yang's homicidal fury.

Over the next four years Yang traveled constantly between the Chinese provinces of Henan, Anhui, Shandong and Hebei, leaving behind a trail of bloody destruction in his wake. His victims were usually farming folk whose homes he entered while they slept. He is known to have carried out 26 such attacks, claiming 67 victims, many of them women and children. On at least two occasions he wiped out entire families.

An attack that clearly illustrates Yang's M.O. occurred on December 6, 2002. The Liu family, Liu Zhanwei, 30, his wife, son, daughter, mother and father were farmers from Liuzhuang Village in Henan's

Xiping County. At the time of the attack they were in the process of moving to a new home and Liu Zhanwei's 68-year-old father Liu Zhongyuan had spent the night at the new residence, which he was readying for the family's arrival.

He returned to the family home the following morning and walked in on a scene of utter carnage. There was blood everywhere. His young granddaughter lay on the ground with a gaping hole in her head that exposed her brain matter. In another room Zhongyuan found his son, daughter-in-law and grandson, all of them brutally bludgeoned to death. Only Zhongyuan's wife was still alive but she'd been so severely beaten that she was entirely paralyzed and could only respond to questions by blinking her eyes. She died in the hospital 10 days later. Police later found a pair of bloody white gloves at the scene, a signature of the "Monster Killer."

The police of course knew by now that a serial killer was rampaging through the provinces. But in common with other serial murder cases in China, the investigation was pitifully inadequate. The police appeared more concerned with protecting the image of the Chinese state than with catching the killer. The media was also prevented from reporting on the crimes. This too was common practice in China when dealing with serial murder cases.

Yang Xinhai might never have been caught but for a chance raid on a nightclub in Cangzhou, Hebei Province on November 3, 2003. One of the officers involved in the operation thought that Yang was behaving suspiciously and therefore took him into custody. Back at the station Yang's prints were run, turning up a match to murder inquiries in Anhui, Shandong and Henan. It was only once DNA testing was carried out that the police realized they'd captured the elusive "Monster Killer."

Yang Xinhai appeared before the Intermediate People's Court in Luohe City on February 1, 2004, and was found guilty after a trial that lasted less than an hour. He was sentenced to death, the sentence carried out by a bullet to the back of the head on February 14.

Miyuki Ishikawa

The Demon Midwife

Miyuki Ishikawa is virtually unknown outside of her native Japan. Yet the "Demon Midwife" is the worst mass murder in Japanese history, responsible for the deaths of at least 103 infants. Even more chilling was her method of murder. She deliberately neglected the helpless babies in her care, allowing them to die a slow and painful death while she tried to extort money from their impoverished parents for services rendered.

Ishikawa was born in Kunitomi, Miyazaki Prefecture, in 1897 and went on to study medicine at Tokyo University. Specializing as a midwife she took up a position at Kotobuki Maternity Hospital, eventually working her way through the ranks to become director of the facility. During this time she also married, although the union produced no children.

Ishikawa at any rate had her hands full with the running of her hospital which was overcrowded and poorly funded. The women who gave birth here were in the main peasant stock, with very little money and usually with many mouths to feed. Many of the children were simply abandoned at the hospital after the mothers gave birth.

For a time Ishikawa sought genuinely to help, approaching social services and various charities for funding. When those requests were turned down she settled on another solution, one as efficient as it was cruel and heartless. She turned to mass infanticide.

It is difficult to understand how someone trained in the care of newborns could carry out such atrocities, but Ishikawa appeared to believe that she was doing good. Her M.O. was to section off certain newborns, those from the most impoverished families, and leave them without care or sustenance until they died of hunger and thirst. The cries of these starving infants must have been horrendous to hear, but Ishikawa paid them no heed and instructed her staff to do the same. Many resigned in protest although amazingly, no one went to the authorities. To add insult to injury, Ishikawa sought to profit from these deaths. She approached the families of the dead children and demanded payment of around 4,000 yen. Her reasoning was that the amount was a pittance compared to the cost of raising a child.

Ishikawa went to great lengths to cover her tracks, paying off a doctor named Shiro Nakayama to issue fake death certificates and paying bribes to various officials.

But the deaths of so many children could not go unnoticed forever, even in a country like Japan where at the time children were considered the "property" of their parents. Eventually two police officers chanced upon five tiny boxes that were found to contain the emaciated corpses of five infants. It was quite obvious that the babies had not died of natural causes and an inquiry was launched.

First the carpenter who had constructed the boxes was traced. He said that he had built the tiny coffins and many more like them for the Kotobuki hospital. He also revealed that he had been taking boxes to a local crematorium when the police had stopped him, a trip he'd made many times before.

The tiny corpses had meanwhile been removed to a local hospital for autopsy, where it was revealed that most had died of malnourishment and that some had also shown signs of pneumonia. The deaths, in the view of the medical examiner, had been deliberately caused. The culprits were not difficult to find. On January 15, 1948, Miyuki Ishikawa was arrested along with her husband and accomplice Takeshi.

With the suspects now in custody, the police expanded their investigation and recovered 70 more corpses scattered across various locations in Shinjuku district, including 30 buried at a local temple. Ishikawa meanwhile was defiant, passing the blame on to irresponsible parents for having children that they could not afford to raise. Surprisingly given the horrific nature of the crimes, public opinion appeared to be on her side.

That argument however was never going to hold up in a court of law. Yet even though she was found guilty of infanticide, the sentence was a ludicrously lenient eight years. Her husband and Dr. Nakayama got just four years in prison and even those sentences were later halved by the Tokyo Superior Court in 1952.

And so it was that Miyuki Ishikawa, the worst mass murderer in Japanese history, served only four years for the murder of over 100 infants. The case did however produce some positive outcomes, with new child protection laws passed and a new national certification system for midwives put in place. As a direct result of the Ishikawa case, Japan also passed a law legalizing abortions for financial reasons.

As for matron Ishikawa, little is known about her life after her release from prison.

Raman Raghav

During the year 1968, the sprawling city of Bombay, India (now Mumbai) existed in a state of virtual siege. A serial killer was stalking the city and preying on the poorest of its citizens, those who lived in ramshackle huts or slept on the sidewalk. All of the victims were bludgeoned to death as they slept, the motive unknown but each attack marked by its extreme overkill.

In August 1968, a new Deputy Commissioner of Police was appointed to the Bombay CID. Ramakant Kulkarni was considered young for such a senior role but he had already established a stellar reputation as an investigator, so much so that he was widely lauded as India's 'Sherlock Holmes.'

Kulkarni immediately made the series of murders his top priority. He soon discovered a similar spate of crimes that had occurred a few years earlier between 1965 and 1966. During that period 19 people had been assaulted as they slept, nine of them succumbing to their injuries. Unfortunately, those who survived were unable to offer any information that might help to catch the killer.

The police however were not without suspects. During a routine patrol along the municipal water line where most of the murders had occurred, officers had picked up a man whose furtive behavior had attracted their attention. The man gave his name as 'Raman Raghav' but the police soon learned that he used several aliases including

'Sindhi Dalwai', 'Talwai', 'Thambi' and 'Veluswami'. They'd also found that he had an extensive police record with nine previous convictions, mostly for theft.

That unfortunately had been insufficient cause to hold the suspect and the police were forced to let him go. The question was, had Raghav returned? Kulkarni believed he had and instructed his officers to find him.

But that was easier said than done. Bombay is a huge city which even back then had a population of millions, many of them homeless and transient. A massive manhunt over several weeks failed to turn up their quarry, although they did eventually track down an old acquaintance of Raghav who admitted that she'd seen him recently.

With confirmation now that Raghav was in Bombay, the police redoubled their efforts. In the meanwhile, a fingerprint lifted from one of the crime scenes proved that Kulkarni was on the right track. It was matched to Raman Raghav.

When Raghav was eventually apprehended, it happened almost by chance. An alert police inspector by the name of Alex Fialho spotted a man matching Raghav's description on the street. The man was wearing a khaki shirt and shorts with what looked like bloodstains on them. When Fialho asked him to identify himself, he said he was Sindhi Dalwai, one of the aliases commonly used by Raghav. Fialho then placed him under arrest.

The police now had their number one suspect in custody but Raghav proved a hard nut to crack. For two days he maintained a stoic silence.

Eventually out of desperation, one of the interrogators tried to win Raghav's favor by asking him if there was anything he wanted. Raghav immediately replied that he wanted Murgi (chicken).

An officer was quickly sent to a nearby restaurant, returning with a plate of chicken curry and rice. In no time at all Raghav had finished the dish and asked for a second helping which was also provided.

The officer then asked if there was anything else he required. "Yes," said Raghav, "I would like hair oil, a comb and a mirror. I would also have liked a prostitute but I guess the law does not permit that while one is in custody."

The comb and a bottle of coconut oil were provided and Raghav massaged the oil into his entire body before combing his hair and then admiring himself in the mirror. He then turned to the officers. "Now tell me what you want," he said.

"We want to know about the murders of course," one of the officers replied.

"Well, I shall tell you all about them," Raghav said. "Get a vehicle, an armed guard and two witnesses. The law requires that."

Raghav was true to his word, first leading the officers to a thorny bush where he revealed his murder weapon, an octagonal iron rod bent at one end and tapering at the other, known as an akada. There were what looked like blood stains on the metal. Raghav also produced knives, a screwdriver, a flashlight and a colored napkin. The napkin he said was his 'loot' from a double homicide.

Next Raghav took his police escort on a tour of the Bombay suburb of Borivili where he produced various items he'd stolen from his victims, including a stove and an umbrella. He then undertook to make a full confession before a magistrate.

The following excerpts from that confession provide a chilling insight into the mind of a killer who regarded murder almost as a mundane every day activity.

"At Poisar, off the Ahmedabad road, I saw a woman and child sleeping inside a hut, where a man was sleeping outside. I hit the man on the head, and he got up shouting. I hit him again till he died. The girl also started shouting and I ran away."

"On the Malad side of the Ahmedabad road, I saw a hamlet and some stables. A bearded Muslim was sleeping on a cot. The door of the hamlet was not locked. I hit him on the way in and he died on the spot. I took his wristwatch and when I saw some money in his jhabba, which was hanging inside, I put the jhabba in my bag. I also took some groundnuts in a bottle, an umbrella and a torch. Once home, I removed the money from the jhabba and tore it to make handkerchiefs."

"A few days later I saw a hut in the same area. I peeped inside and saw a woman and a child. She was wearing a gold necklace. I kept watch until one day I found her sleeping and her husband beside her. I cut the string that fastened the front door and then hit the man with an iron rod until he died. The woman and child were shouting and I hit them both and killed them. I was thinking of sleeping with the woman but someone came and I ran away. The gold necklace turned out to be imitation gold."

Raman Raghav went on trial for his crimes in July 1969. Found guilty he was initially sentenced to death, although the sentence was later commuted to life in prison after he was diagnosed with chronic paranoid schizophrenia and found to be 'incurably mentally ill.' He died of kidney failure at Pune's Sassoon Hospital in 1987.

Shinichirou Azuma

The Kobe School Killer

On the morning of Tuesday, May 27, 1997, a janitor arrived to begin his shift at a junior high school in Kobe, Japan. He was just about to enter the premises when he spotted a box sitting on the sidewalk in front of the main school gates. The box was not wrapped and so it was obviously not a delivery. What then was it doing there? Curious as to what it might contain the janitor approached, peeled back the top flaps and peered inside. He instantly wished that he hadn't. The box contained a severed head.

The police were called and rushed to the school, getting there just in time to cordon off the area before the first students arrived. Forensics officers then began examining the box and its macabre contents. The head was that of a child and the detectives in attendance thought that they knew who it belonged to. Eleven-year-old Jun Hase had disappeared from a nearby elementary school three days earlier. The boy suffered from mild retardation and it had originally been believed that he'd wandered off and got lost. Now the police knew different.

As the day progressed officers fanned out through the area, conducting a search in the hope of locating the rest of the boy's body. It was found eventually, crammed under an abandoned house in woods near the school. Multiple stab wounds to the torso seemed to suggest that the child had been stabbed to death, while abrasions on the neck indicated that the head had been removed with a hand saw.

By now the police had a new twist to contend with. While examining the severed head, a pathologist had found a note crammed into the victim's mouth. "This is the beginning of the game," it read. "You police guys stop me if you can." The author went on to boast that he "desperately wanted to see people die" and that he was exacting revenge for his "years of great bitterness." The note concluded with the misspelled English words "shooll kill." It was signed, "The School Killer."

The police took the threats very seriously indeed. In fact, they were by now convinced that Jun Hase was not the killer's first victim. Just two weeks earlier a ten-year-old girl named Ayaka Yamashita had been found bludgeoned to death near the same school that Jun Hase had attended. Three other young girls had also been attacked but had survived to provide police with a description of their assailant. Detectives had been uncertain of what to make of those descriptions. The girls had insisted that the attacker was a "schoolboy." But could a child really be responsible for such atrocities? Much as they did not want to believe it, the authorities had to take that line of inquiry seriously.

On June 6 a letter arrived at the offices of a local newspaper. Claiming to be from the "School Killer," it issued a new threat. Three people a week were to be killed. "I am putting my life at stake for the sake of this game," the author wrote. "If I'm caught, I'll probably be hanged. The police should be angrier and more tenacious in pursuing me. It is only when I give pain to people that I can ease my own pain."

The letter was signed differently this time. It was attributed to "Seito Sakakibara," which the writer claimed was his real name. Inquiries into the name however came up blank, although they did lead police to a possible suspect, a 14-year-old junior high student named Shinichirou Azuma.

Azuma was taken into custody on June 28. And his involvement in the Kobe school killings was soon confirmed when the police found his diary, which described in graphic detail the two murders and the attacks on the three little girls. Much of this disturbing journal has been withheld from the public but that which has been released provides a chilling depiction of a young psychopath.

Azuma shows all of the classic signs of the fledgling serial killer. He talks gleefully of mutilating cats, beheading pigeons and riding over frogs with his bicycle. He speaks of his love of weapons. "I can ease my irritation when I'm holding a survival knife or spinning scissors like a pistol," he expounds. The entry for May 16, the day that he attacked two of his juvenile victims reads: "I carried out sacred experiments today to confirm how fragile human beings are. I brought the hammer down when the girl turned to face me. I think I hit her a few times but I was too excited to remember." And in true serial killer fashion he rages against society, in particular the Japanese school system which he blames for everything that was wrong in his life.

Of course Azuma was never going to have to deal with the consequences of his killing spree. At just 14 years of age he could not be tried for murder or even be publicly named. Instead he appeared before a judge under the title "Child A" and was committed to a 'medical reformatory' where he was to undergo treatment for his sexual sadism and compulsion to kill. In 2003, having served just six years, he was declared cured of these afflictions. On March 10, 2004, he was paroled. He'd spend the next 18 months under supervised parole. In December 2004 he dropped out of sight and disappeared.

However, although his whereabouts remain a secret, Azuma was not about to forfeit the infamy his horrific crimes had given him. In 2015, he released a book titled Zekka, written under the same alias he'd used during his killing spree, Seito Sakakibara. In it he describes himself as an "incorrigible sexual deviant" who had taken grim satisfaction in harming animals and ultimately in killing human beings. The book was a bestseller. That same year Azuma started a website, which again focuses on his crimes and his motivation for committing them. The site features bizarre graphics of a masked man (presumably Azuma) who is sometimes depicted with the body of a scorpion.

Azuma claims that the book and website are his way of showing remorse for his actions. Given what we know about this type of killer, one would be justified in skepticism.

Kanae Kijima

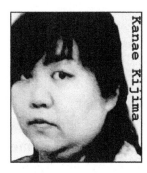

Naoki Yasuda had signed up for the internet dating site more in hope than expectation. He didn't see why any attractive single woman would need to resort to such means in order to attract a partner. And if such a woman did, he couldn't see why she'd be interested in a shy lifelong bachelor like him. Still he was lonely and desperate for female company so he posted up his details and to his surprise soon had a response.

The woman's name was Kanae Kijima and she was just what Naoki was looking for, someone who described herself as a homebody interested in a serious relationship. At 34 she was 12 years younger than Naoki and if her picture was anything to go by, quite pretty. A date was quickly set up at a local restaurant.

Naoki was somewhat disappointed at his first sighting of Kanae. She was considerably plainer and sturdier than the flattering picture she'd posted on the dating site. But those initial reservations were swept away once they got talking. Kanae was kind, soft-spoken and attentive and she seemed genuinely interested in starting a serious relationship. A few more dates and the pair were talking about setting up home together. In September 2009 Kanae moved out of her modest Tokyo apartment and into Naoki's house in nearby Chiba Prefecture.

Over the next three weeks Naoki could hardly believe his luck at landing such a gem. His new partner was an attentive and loving companion, a spectacular cook and an extremely diligent housekeeper. There were three cooked meals a day and cups of tea delivered at regular intervals without him having to ask. The home was kept spotless without him having to lift a finger to help. Even after such a short courtship, Naoki began thinking seriously about asking Kanae to be his wife. She seemed almost too good to be true.

Then on September 21, after three blissful weeks of cohabitation, a bombshell was dropped on Naoki's newfound happiness. The police arrived to take Kanae into custody. Bewildered, Naoki asked about the charges. The answer stunned him. Kanae had been meeting men on internet chat sites, drugging and then robbing them. And that wasn't the worst of it. Four men had died. Kanae Kijima it appeared was a new breed of serial killer, an internet Black Widow.

At first Naoki refused to believe the allegations. Kanae had seemed so genuine, so caring, so trustworthy. But as the details of the case came to light he was forced to reassess his position. His loving companion it appeared was a fraudster of epic proportions. She'd been at this for a while, defrauding dozens of men while posing as a prospective marriage partner, a home-helper or a therapist.

According to police reports, she preyed mainly on lonely middle-aged men who she found by trawling konkatsu (marriage-hunting) websites. Her little enterprise had netted her 200-million yen ($1.8m) in just a couple of years. Naoki Yasuda had been lucky to escape with his life.

Kanae Kijima's first victim was Sadao Fukuyama. The 70-year-old was the manager of a recycling shop, a thrifty careful man who was said to have a healthy suspicion of strangers. And yet Fukuyama was no match for Kijima's persuasive wiles. After luring the elderly man via a dating site, she'd spun him a tale of woe. She had been a promising pianist she said, but had been forced to give up her studies after her parents were killed in a plane crash, leaving her destitute. Her greatest wish was to complete her music degree. Fukuyama, so careful in his pecuniary affairs was apparently taken in. He handed over 3.2 million yen ($30,000) to cover Kijima's tuition fees. Then a couple of months into the relationship he went even further, handing over his bank card and PIN number. Kijima then proceeded to drain his account of 74 million yen ($680,000).

Sadao Fukuyama was found dead at his home on August 6, 2007. Because of his advanced age the police did not suspect foul play at the time, although they'd later have cause to revise that assumption.

The next man to fall victim to the heartless killer was even older than Sadao Fukuyama. Kenzo Ando was an 80-year-old invalid who Kijima contacted via a website advertising for home carers. Posing as a nurse, Kijima insinuated herself into the pensioner's life and managed to coax his bank card and PIN number out of him.

She then drugged Ando and set his house on fire, hoping that the blaze would obliterate the evidence. However, the fire department was able to extinguish the flames before they could consume Mr. Ando's body. His bloodstream was found to contain traces of a sedative. Meanwhile a check on the deceased's financial affairs revealed that 1.8 million yen ($20,000) had been withdrawn from his bank account in the days leading up to his death.

Not all of Kanae Kijima's victims ended up dead. The lucky ones were simply duped out of their money before the heavyset temptress left them in the lurch and moved on to new targets. However, she did not hesitate to kill if a mark cottoned on to her game or perhaps demanded the repayment of a "loan."

A typical case was that of 53-year-old Takao Terada, found dead of carbon monoxide poisoning in his Tokyo home in February 2009. Kijima had reeled Terada in by telling him a sob story about a cake shop that she had planned on opening. At the last moment she said, her backer had pulled out, leaving her in the lurch and deep in debt. A sum of 2.4 million yen would get her back on track. In exchange, she promised to cut Terada in on a share of the profits from the business. The money was in her account the next day. The day after, Takao Terada was dead.

Kanae Kijima had thus far managed to commit at least three murders and countless frauds and yet somehow fly below police radars. Most of her living victims were embarrassed about being so easily duped and as for the dead well, dead men tell no tales. But with her next murder Kijima would finally overstep the mark, leading to her eventual arrest.

Yoshiyuki Oide was typical of the sort of men that Kijima preyed on. A shy and lonely 41-year-old, Oide's hobby was building model tanks. He kept a blog on which he posted pictures of his creations, usually with a description and history of the vehicle in question. But on August 2, he oddly broke the pattern to post something personal.

"At 41, I've found someone and I'm going to meet her family, so I may not be able to write as much," he announced. "We're talking about buying a house and starting a new life together. I'll be going on a three-day trip with my fiancé before the wedding."

On 6 August Oide's corpse was found slumped across the back seat of a rented car in Tokyo's northern suburbs. Beside him lay a charcoal burner, commonly used as a means of suicide in Japan. However, something about the scene did not sit right with investigators. For starters, the keys were missing from the ignition. Who had taken them? Then an autopsy revealed that although Oide had died of carbon monoxide poisoning, there were traces of a sedative in his bloodstream. Then there was Oide's demeanor in the days leading up to his death. The excited post about his pending marriage did not appear to be the action of someone who was contemplating suicide. Finally, there was motive, 5 million yen ($46,000) removed from the victim's bank account. The police immediately launched a search for Yoshiyuki Oide's mysterious fiancé. It led them eventually to the doorstep of Kanae Kijima's latest conquest, Naoki Yasuda.

Kijima was initially charged with 12 counts of fraud. But the murder of Yoshiyuki Oide was added to the docket after investigators raided Kijima's apartment and found several types of sedative drug, including the type used to incapacitate Oide. Kijima was subsequently indicted for two additional murders, those of Takao Terada and Kenzo Ando.

But the case against Kijima was far from solid. She readily admitted fraud but denied murder, saying that Ando had died of natural causes and that Oide and Terada had taken their own lives after she'd ended her relationships with them. The prosecutor countered by branding her a serial killer and demanding the death penalty. After a trial that lasted 100 days, the judge came down on the side of the prosecution.

On April 13, 2012, Kanae Kijima was found guilty and sentenced to death. She currently awaits execution.

The case has been widely debated in Japan. In a country where women still traditionally occupy a subservient role, Kanae Kijima represents a new kind of monster. And the impact on Japan's thriving internet dating model has been palpable. "How many more Kijimas are out there?" one popular blogger wrote. "It's terrifying."

Huang Yong

On November 11, 2003, a 16-year-old schoolboy named Zhang Liang walked into a police station in Dahuangzhuang village, Henan province China. He had an interesting tale to tell. According to Liang, he'd been playing games at a video arcade four days earlier when a man had approached him. The man told Liang that he was a video game developer and had invented a new game called "God Riding on a Wooden Horse." He invited Liang back to his apartment to play the game. Liang, being a gaming enthusiast, could hardly refuse.

Once they reached the apartment, the man (who identified himself as Yong) showed him a wooden table (actually a noodle-processing device) which he called his "intelligent hobbyhorse." He told the boy that the game had to be played while strapped to the table and so Liang allowed himself to be tied up.

What followed was a nightmare lasting four days, during which Liang was left strapped to the table, repeatedly strangled into unconsciousness and then revived. During this time his abductor kept him alive by feeding him noodles but he assured Liang that he should expect to die eventually. "I've killed 25 people," he said. "You will be number 26."

One can only imagine the terror the young boy must have endured. Yet he kept his cool and made a point of engaging his captor in conversation. Eventually he convinced Yong to let him go by promising that he would take care of him in his old age. Once free, Liang went straight to the police.

At first the officers were reluctant to believe Liang's story. They shouldn't have been. Over the previous three years, from September 2001 to November 2003, upwards of 17 young boys had gone missing from the streets of Dahuangzhuang. Most of them had last been seen alive at Internet Cafes and Gaming Arcades. And yet despite an outcry from parents as the toll of the missing grew, the police simply refused to act, insisting they could not start an investigation without a body. The frustrated parents had eventually banded together and traveled to Beijing in order to demand action. Only then was an official inquiry launched. It had made little headway by the time Liang escaped.

On November 23, a full 12 days after Liang's escape, the police finally called on Huang Yong's home. A search of the premises turned up the table the boy had described as well as an array of leather belts and an extensive collection of violent videos. However, it was the excavation of the back yard that finally revealed the true extent of Yong's murder spree. There, police uncovered the decomposing remains of 17 young boys and men.

Once in custody Yong had no reluctance to confessing. He said that he'd wanted to be an assassin since childhood and that the murders had allowed him to fulfill that dream. But as he spoke it was clear that this wasn't his only motive. Yong said that he strapped the boys to the table and then strangled them with a rope, sometimes reviving them several times before killing them. He then had sex with the corpse, before dissected it and burying it in the garden. The belts the police had found were souvenirs he'd kept from his victims.

Huang Yong went on trial for murder in December 2003. Found guilty, he was sentenced to death, that sentence carried out by a bullet to the back of the head on December 26, 2003.

But the well-deserved death of Huang Yong does not tell the full story. For years the Chinese authorities have insisted that serial killers do not exist in China, a quite ludicrous claim when you consider such recently executed monsters as Zhang Yongming, Duan Guocheng and Yang Xinhai. In each of these cases the investigations had been hampered by official denials, indifference and incompetence. But none of these cases were as badly handled as that of Huang Yong, where despite 17 disappearances from the tiny village, despite the pleas of distraught parents, the police simply refused to act.

Five officials including the chief of police lost their jobs as a result of the scandal. It brought scant consolation to 17 grieving families.

The Rajendra Jakkal Gang

Rajendra Jakkal, Dilip Sutar, Shantaram Jagtap and Munawar Shah were commercial art students at a college in Pune, India. The youths were all from middle-class backgrounds but they had acquired a somewhat unsavory reputation around the college campus. They were drunks, bullies and troublemakers and they were reputed to have robbed several of their fellow students at knifepoint.

Jakkal was the de facto leader of the gang and in January 1976 he hit on an idea to make some easy money. The plan was to kidnap a fellow student named Prakash Hegde and hold him for ransom.

On the afternoon of January 15 the foursome, along with another student Suhas Chandak, put their scheme into action. Luring Prakash to a tin shack on Karve Road, they overpowered him and forced him to write a letter to his father stating that he was leaving home. That same night they took the youth to Peshwe Park Lake where they strangled him with a length of rope. They then placed the body in a steel drum, weighed it down with large stones and submerged it in the lake.

The following day Prakash's father Sundar Hegde received two pieces of correspondence, a ransom demand and the letter from Prakash. Sundar was immediately suspicious as the letter was signed 'Prakash' rather than 'Devdas,' the name by which his family normally called him. He took both the ransom note and the letter to the police but they refused to take it seriously, putting it down to a prank.

The Jakkal gang meanwhile had moved on to new atrocities. On the night of October 31, Jakkal and Sutar forced their way into a Pune home at knifepoint. Achyut Joshi and his wife Usha were robbed and strangled. Then when their teenaged son arrived home unexpectedly, he too was overpowered, beaten and strangled to death. The gang's take from this triple murder was a few thousand rupees, a watch and a mangala (a sacred necklace given by a groom to his bride in Hindu wedding ceremonies).

On November 22 Jakkal and Sutar, still working without the other gang members, broke into the home of Yashomati Bafna. This time however they met their match. The woman and her two servants fought them off and they were forced to retreat, nursing lumps and bruises.

Cowered by this experience, Jakkal called up reinforcements for his next caper. On December 1, all four gang members arrived at the home of 88-year-old Kashinath Shastri Abhyankar, a noted Sanskrit scholar. Also in the home were Abhyankar's wife Indirabai, 76, the couple's maid Sakubai Wagh, 60, and two grandchildren, Jai, aged 21 and Dhananjay, 19.

Forcing their way in the gang soon overpowered the residents, pushed rolls of cloth into their mouths to stifle their cries and tied them up. They then systematically began strangling their victims until only Jai remained alive. The terrified woman was stripped naked, then forced to lead the gang to valuables in the house. Then after ransacking the residence, they killed Jai too.

News of the latest massacre hit the streets the following day, sending Pune into a panic. That evening saw the streets of the city all but deserted, with citizens arming themselves and barricading themselves in their homes. As much as Jakkal and his gang relished the fear they'd sown, it left them with a problem. With the city's populace on high alert, where were they going to find their next victim?

They solved the problem by targeting someone who knew and trusted them, Anil Gokhale, the brother of one of their fellow art students.

On the evening of March 23, 1977, Anil was supposed to meet his brother at a local movie theater. But he was unable to find his sibling at the venue and eventually left. He was walking home when Rajendra Jakkal pulled over and offered him a ride on his motorcycle. Anil happily accepted but instead of taking the boy home, Jakkal rode him to the same tin shack where Prakash Hegde had been murdered. There the rest of the gang waited.

Anil Gokhale was strangled to death with a length of nylon rope, his body tied to a steel ladder and dumped in the Mula-Mutha River. But the gang had done a less than thorough job of disposal. The corpse surfaced the following day and the police noticed that the knots used to tie it to the ladder were similar to those they'd seen in the Joshi and Abhyankar massacres.

Then the police learned that Anil Gokhale had been seen in the company of Rajendra Jakkal the previous evening and Jakkal and the rest of his gang were brought in for questioning.

Interrogated separately, the gang members told conflicting stories, the only common thread being that they had nothing to do with any of the murders. One particularly telling piece of testimony came from Rajendra Jakkal himself. He insisted that he had nothing to do with the Prakash Hegde murder. The investigators were stunned. They weren't aware that Hegde had been killed. They were still treating it as a missing person case.

Jakkal's admission went a long way to convincing the police that he and his gang were behind the killing spree. But it still didn't amount to evidence of murder and as none of the gang members were talking, the police were forced to let them go. They did however keep them under surveillance.

Detectives meanwhile began questioning students at the art college, focusing particularly on known associates of the four suspects. This strategy produced an almost immediate result. One of the youths Satish Gore broke down under police interrogation and confessed what he knew about the murders.

Gore had not been a participant in the crimes but the gang members had told him about them. His testimony led the police to Suhas Chandak, who had witnessed the Hegde killing. Once Chandak told his story, the Jakkal gang was finished.

The deadly foursome were arrested on March 30, 1977. Faced with the fresh evidence against them they quickly confessed, each trying to deflect guilt onto the others. It did them no good. On September 28, 1978, Rajendra Jakkal, Dilip Sutar, Shantaram Jagtap and Munawar Shah were found guilty of murder and sentenced to hang.

They were executed at Yerawada Central Jail on November 27, 1983.

Kiyoshi Okubo

Given its massive population, serial murders are a rarity in Japan. But they are by no means unheard of. In the 1920's a vicious killer named Sataro Fukiage went to the gallows for the murders of seven children; twenty years later a psychopath by the name of Kodaira Yoshio met the same fate for the brutal rape-slayings of 10 women. There are others too, Matsunaga, Nakamura, Miyazaki among them. And then there was Kiyoshi Okubo, perhaps better categorized as a spree killer after a manic 64 days during which he slaughtered eight women.

Kiyoshi Okubo was born on January 17, 1935, the youngest son in a family of eight children. His mother was half Russian and the young boy was teased mercilessly at school over his "western" appearance. Perhaps to compensate for this his parents lavished all of their children with affection, with Kiyoshi his mother's favorite.

From an early age the boy had problems at school, with poor grades and even worse discipline. He was regularly censured for his lack of respect towards teachers, his overtly sexual behavior towards female students and his vulgar utterances.

And his aberrant behavior was not restricted to the classroom and schoolyard. In the summer of 1946, at the age of just 11, Okubo was caught trying to molest a neighbor's four-year-old daughter. This earned him the neighborhood nickname "little Kodaira," after the notorious serial killer mentioned above.

Nine years on and Okubo graduated to the real thing when he was arrested for raping a 17-year-old high school student in Maebashi. That earned him an 18- month prison term, although the sentence was almost immediately commuted to three years' probation. Arrested on a second rape charge five months later, he found the judge somewhat less merciful. That offense earned him three years at Matsumoto Prison.

Okubo was paroled in 1960 but the years inside had taught him nothing. Adopting the alias "Watanabe Kyoshi," he registered as a student, a ruse designed to put him in close proximity with college coeds.

Okubo married in May 1962 and had fathered two children by the time of his next arrest in February 1967. This time the charges related to an attack on two young women and earned him four and a half years inside.

He was released on March 2, 1971. Ten days later he bought himself a cream-colored Mazda sedan and began trolling again for victims. Less than two weeks later he launched his final murderous rampage.

Nobody knows what spurred Okubo into this onslaught. What is known is that over the next two months he accosted more than 150 women, raping over a dozen and killing eight.

The first to die was a 17-year-old high school student Tsuda Miyako, raped and strangled to death on March 31, 1971. Ten days later Oikawa Mieko, a 17-year-old waitress was murdered. On April 17 it was 19-year-old Ida Chieko, a day later Kawabata Shigeko, 17, another student.

The police were by now tracking Okubo with reported sightings of his vehicle coming in by the hour. Okubo for his part made little attempt at subterfuge. It was almost as though he were issuing a "catch me if you can" challenge to his pursuers.

And still the body count kept rising. Seventeen-year-old student Sato Akemi was raped and murdered on April 27. Five days later Kawabo Kazuyo, an 18-year-old telephone operator met a brutal end at Okubo's hands. Less than a week after that Takemura Reiko, 21, was slain. The following day 21-year-old housemaid Takahashi Naoko was savagely murdered.

On the evening of May 14, the police received a reported sighting of Okubo's vehicle in the Takasaki neighborhood. Officers immediately raced to the scene and found the fugitive sitting in his car with a young woman. On his arrest, Okubo reportedly handed the woman some money and said "You'd better take a taxi home."

Okubo had no problem admitting to his crimes, indeed he seemed eager to provide graphic details of the rapes and murders he'd committed. The fault he said lay not with him but with the police. The way they'd treated him after his previous arrests had led him to become a "brute" and a "rebel against authority."

Convicted and sentenced to death on February 22, 1973, Okubo spent the next three years appealing his sentence. His appeals rejected, he was finally hanged at Tokyo's Kosuge Detention Center on January 23, 1976. He went reluctantly to the gallows, apparently having to be carried the final few yards.

Yoo Young-chul

The Chaser

By his own reckoning, Yoo Young-chul had never been given a fair shake in life. For starters he'd been born into a family plagued by a history of epilepsy. Both his father and older brother had died from the affliction while in their thirties and Yoo would tell anyone who would listen that he didn't expect to live beyond his 40th birthday.

But while Yoo could do nothing about his medical condition, he could do something about the other problem in his life. Born into poverty, he was deeply resentful at the inequality between the haves and have-nots. His response was to set about redressing this imbalance through a life of crime.

Yoo was not a successful criminal and served 14 terms in prison for various thefts and other offenses. In between these periods of incarceration he managed to marry and father a son. However, after he was jailed for the rape of a child in 2000, his wife divorced him.

By the time he emerged from prison in 2003, Yoo was a bitter man determined to take revenge on society. At least 21 people would die to sate his anger.

Yoo's initial targets were wealthy older people, living in the affluent areas of southern Seoul. His M.O. was to break in during daylight hours when younger family members were at work, leaving the older residents at his mercy.

On September 24, 2003, he entered a house in the Seoul suburb of Sinsa-dong and beat to death a retired 73-year old university professor and his 68-year-old wife. Less than two weeks later on October 9, he raided a home in Seodaemun-gu, killing three family members including an 85-year-old woman.

One month later he broke into a southern Seoul home and killed a wealthy financier and his wife, both 69. On November 4 he committed a triple homicide in the same area, killing the 87-year-old homeowner, a 53-year-old maid and a baby. He then set fire to the apartment.

With the police now heavy on the ground in south Seoul, Yoo changed both tack and victim profile. As would later emerge, this was not due to cleverness on his part but rather due to another incident that sparked his ire. He had been dating a prostitute and had asked her to marry him. Angered by the woman's refusal, he turned his murderous attentions to others of her kind.

Over the next five months Yoo murdered no fewer than eleven women, all of them escorts, bar hostesses or masseuses. His modus operandi seldom varied. He'd pick a woman up and bring her back to his studio apartment in Nogosan-dong. After having sex with the woman, Yoo would bludgeon her to death with a hammer, then dismember her body and pack it into plastic garbage bags. The bags would then be taken to an isolated mountainous area near Yonsei University where they would be interred in a shallow grave. According to Yoo's later confession he cannibalized four of his victims, eating their livers. He said that eating human flesh "refreshed" him.

By Yoo's own admission he would have gone on killing indefinitely, but as so often happens in serial killer cases, it was a victim who escaped his clutches that led to his downfall.

Arrested on July 15 for beating a prostitute, he managed to squirm free and escape his pursuers. He was recaptured 12 hours later at Yongdungpo subway station. Police found in his possession a fake police identification card and a pair of handcuffs.

But the police did not yet know who they had arrested. It was only once Yoo started talking that they realized they'd captured the monster who had been terrorizing their city, the most deadly serial killer in South Korea's history.

Yoo soon led the police to his dumping ground where they recovered the dismembered and decomposing remains of 11 women. He confessed also to the south Seoul killings as well as murders in the western port city of Inchon and in Buson.

A search of Yoo's apartment produced nothing incriminating but told its own story of an obsessively neat man who collected scrapbooks with pictures of cars, holidays and other luxury items.

Yoo Young-chul went on trial in November 2004, charged with 21 counts of murder. Found guilty, he was sentenced to death. As South Korea currently has a moratorium on capital punishment it is unlikely that the sentence will ever be carried out.

Zhang Yongming

The Cannibal Monster

China has a long history of cannibalism. In the 4th century for example, it was quite common for harem girls to be slaughtered and served up as a delicacy to guests, while during the Tang Dynasty of the 7th and 8th centuries, enemy soldiers were routinely used as a food source for an army on the march. In the 13th century, Marco Polo returned to Italy from his Far East expeditions with horror stories about human flesh consumption. And as recently as the 1800's, there were restaurants in China that served nothing but human flesh. More recently, the Communist state's disastrous "Great Leap Forward" of the late 50's and early 60's drove millions of ordinary citizens to cannibalism in order to survive.

China has also produced its fair share of cannibalistic killers, most notably Zhang Yongming, the so-called "Cannibal Monster." Over a period of four years from 2008 to 2012, Yongming strangled and dismembered at least 12 youths in the tiny village of Nanmen, later selling their dried flesh as "ostrich meat" in the local market.

Little is known about Zhang's early life. We first learn of his existence in 1979 when he was arrested for killing a man and mutilating his corpse. A conviction in that case saw him sentenced to death but the punishment was subsequently reduced to life imprisonment. Paroled in September 1997 after serving just 16 years, Yongming was relocated to Nanmen in southwest China's Yunnan province. There he was given a tract of land and a meager government stipend and promptly forgotten about.

Zhang kept mostly to himself and exchanged hardly a word with anyone in the village. For their part the villagers appear to have regarded him as a local eccentric who was best avoided. That is until young men and teenaged boys started going missing from the village.

At first the distraught parents thought that their sons had been kidnapped to work as slave labor in the brick quarries. However, their appeals to local authorities brought a tepid response at best and self-funded inquiries fared no better. Despite several of the parents spending their entire life savings to find their sons, not a single one of the missing boys was located. They seemed simply to have vanished.

There were rumors of course, clues even. Like the mysterious green garbage bags seen hanging outside Yongming's shack. Someone said they'd seen bones protruding from the bags, but no one seriously suspected the dim-witted farmer or the suspicious looking dried meat he sold at market.

Had any of the villagers known about Yongming's murderous past, they might have taken it more seriously when he looped a leather belt around a youth's neck in December 2011. Villagers who heard 17-year-old Zhang Jianyuan's screams and came rushing to his aid found Yongming with the belt drawn tightly around the boy's throat. The police were called but Yongming laughed off the incident, insisting that he was only playing a prank on the boy. They believed him. Remarkably given the spate of disappearances of young men from the area and Yongming's previous conviction for a mutilation murder, the police did not even bother searching his house.

But even in a repressive country like China, the disappearances of over a dozen boys and young men from an area that spanned only two square miles could not be kept under wraps forever. Word eventually leaked to the media and stories began to appear in the local press. These articles did not suggest that a serial killer was at large, but they did put pressure on the Ministry of Public Security to take action. As a result a team of investigators was sent to Nanmen. They almost immediately picked up a pattern to the disappearances. All of the victims had gone missing along a particular stretch of road, a path that led directly past Yongming's house.

The investigators started checking locations and talking to homeowners along the route. In the course of those inquiries, they began to hear stories about the mysterious garbage bags hanging outside Yongming's home. According to at least one local, the bones they contained were human.

The investigative team laughed off those reports as superstitious nonsense but as Yongming's home was along the route anyway, they decided to pay him a visit. They were in for a shock. The bags were hanging from Yongming's porch as described. They did contain bones and those bones were unquestionably human.

After taking Yongming into custody, the officers carried out a search of his humble wooden shack. They were unprepared for what they found. Grisly chunks of human flesh hung from hooks where they'd been left to dry; on a counter sat three large jars, each one containing human eyeballs floating in a semi-opaque fluid; there were more bones scattered around the house and more still buried in a vegetable garden, which also held the decaying flesh of several of Yongming's victims. Under interrogation, Yongming admitted that he subsisted almost exclusively on human flesh and also fed it to his dogs. What he couldn't eat he salted and dried, selling it at the local market as "ostrich jerky."

Despite its lurid nature, Yongming's story was not the media sensation it might have been. The Chinese government denies the existence of serial killers within its borders and regulates the reporting of such cases. Another aspect of the case however did cause a media storm, the story of the utterly incompetent handling of the inquiry by the local police. Twenty people had gone missing from a tiny hamlet within the space of just two years. Yet with citizens up in arms, with local chatter rife about Yongming's activities, with Yongming's previous murder rap and arrest for trying to strangle a young man, the police did nothing. A judicial inquiry was launched into the case and would ultimately result in 12 local officials including the police chief losing their jobs.

Zhang Yongming meanwhile went on trial and was unsurprisingly found guilty of murder and sentenced to death. This time there would be no reprieve for the depraved cannibal. On January 10, 2013, the state-run Xinhua News Agency carried a curt report. It stated that Yongming had been "escorted to a place of execution and executed."

For more True Crime books by Robert Keller please visit

http://bit.ly/kellerbooks

Made in the USA
Coppell, TX
17 September 2020

38011737R00079